Women and the Koran

Bernard Payeur

Front Cover

The front cover is from a photograph by John Goddard of the Toronto Star which has been embossed for artistic purposes and to obscure the identity of the participants in a prayer in the cafeteria of a Toronto, Ontario (Canada) public school.

At the very top of the picture are prostrated boys and men. Behind them it is women and girls.

At the bottom of the cover you can make out school girls sitting and watching. They cannot participate in the prayer because they are menstruating, and in the eyes of Allah are unclean.

ISBN: 978-0-9918655-8-1

Note for Librarians: A cataloguing record for this book is available from Library and Archives Canada at www.collectionscanada.gc.ca/amicus/index-e.html

Boreal Books
www.boreal.ca

These are the exalted cranes,
Whose intercession [with Allah] is to be hoped for.

To the memory of al-Lat, al-Uzza and
Manat, and all that was lost when their
existence was denied.

*Women and the Koran is largely an excerpt from Pain,
Pleasure and Prejudice, a comprehensive review of the Koran.*

Other extracts from Pain, Pleasure and Prejudice

Shared Prophets

Getting to Know Allah

The Islamic Hereafter

Allah's War Against the Unbelievers

From Merchant to Messenger

Contents

Foreword

It was late Tuesday night and the place was not very busy. It was not because it was Tuesday at Thursdays. Thursdays was usually busy every day of the week, but there was a raging snow storm outside when she walked in, the most stunning black woman I had ever seen.

It was only a matter of time before our eyes met, and when they did, I said hi, and she said hello. I said bonjour, she said bonsoir. She asked if she could move closer. I said *bien sûr*. She spoke near perfect French, not that high pitch, hysterical, pretentious French spoken by Parisian snobs and garçons de café, but a happy, melodious French, not unlike in tone to the English that you might hear on a beach in Jamaica.

When it was time to leave I offered to walk her to her car. When we got outside the snow had really piled up. My hotel was just across the street. She asked if she could park her car in the underground parking lot of the Chateau Royale and spend the night. I agreed.

I think it was when we were alone in the elevator that she mentioned that if we got to know each other better, there would be a price to pay – got to feed the kids. I had not been born the day before. The relationship would mature, but not necessarily the way that is already being played out in your minds.

I wanted to know about the world she had left behind. I remember the first time I asked her about her home in Africa. We were having dinner at Thursday's second floor restaurant, outside, on the patio, on a warm summer evening. I wanted to hear about the lions, the tigers, the tropical rain forest, the endless summers...

She laughed. Her country was not like that at all. It was dirt roads, arid dusty fields, no wildlife to speak of and, as far as the tropical forest was concerned, there was almost none left.

At other times, not that night, she talked about her family. Her father and mother remained in Africa. She hinted at a relationship which seems to have been her prime motivator in immigrating to Canada; and that was to escape a marriage in the Islamic tradition, which she once described as "god-sanctioned rape."

Twelve years ago a young black women from Africa who preferred prostituting herself on the cold streets of Montreal rather than enter into an arranged marriage got me interested in the Koran.

She opened my eyes. It is my hope that *Women and the Koran* will do the same for you.

September 2012

Revelations and Generalizations

Revelations and Generalizations is the opening explanatory chapter of *Pain, Pleasure and Prejudice. What is written there about the why, the wherefore and the methodology used in that ground-breaking publication is applicable to Women and the Koran.*

THE PEOPLE
114 An-Nâs

In the Name of Allah,
the Compassionate, the Merciful

114:1 Say: "I seek refuge with the Lord of the People,

114:2 "The King of the people,

114:3 "The God of the people,

114:5 "From the evil of the slinking whisperer [Satan],

114:6 "Who whispers in the breasts of people,

114:7 "Both jinn and men."

Both jinn and men! That is it, the last verse of the Koran. What a read! What a revelation! What is a jinn? Jinns are spirits that inhabit another dimension. There are good and evil jinns. The caricature of the genie is probably based on this creature of the Koran.

When I decided to read and study the Koran with the intention of writing about it, I was determined to get a Muslim's interpretation, an interpretation that could only be viewed as being favourable to Islam. I also wanted a translation that was easy to read and understand. The translation that seemed to satisfy these requirements was an interpretation by Majid Fakhry, Emeritus Professor of Philosophy at the American University of Beirut, which has the seal of approval of Al-Azhar University of Egypt, a world-renowned center for Islamic study for more than 900 years.

> Messrs Garnet Publishing Limited, with reference to your letter dated 5 July, 2000, in respect of your request that this department (Islamic Research) may review your book titled: An Interpretation of the Qur'an, English Translation of the Meanings. A Bilingual Edition translated by Majid Fakhry.

> After having reviewed this book as requested we have the pleasure to declare that we have no objection to approve this book and put it in circulation or introduced for republication.

> *Islamic Research Academy, Al-Azhar University*

In the translator's own words "we have tried to express ourselves in a simple, readable English idiom." Publishers weekly wrote of Fakhry's notable accomplishment: "Succeeds in expressing the meanings of the original Arabic in simple readable English."

My goals in reading the Koran were diverse. At the top of my list was gaining an understanding of what makes this book so special; to understand what makes the religion based on its content so attractive to so many, and yes, to satisfy my curiosity about what God sounds like, or more accurately, reads like. I also read the Koran in the hope of dispelling some prejudices and apprehensions that I had developed after reading about Islam from authors, devoted Muslims most of them, who had mostly nothing but praise for Allah and His "perfect religion".

The *Final Draft* of Pain, Pleasure and Prejudice is the culmination of almost ten years of work and study. I believe it is the most honest, forthright, complete review ever attempted by a non-Muslim of Allah's and His anointed Messenger's legacy: the Koran. This appraisal takes Allah and the Prophet Muhammad at their word, as does most of the Muslim world, and so should you. Although I consider myself well versed (no pun intended) in the Koran and the life and times of the Prophet Muhammad, in Pain, Pleasure and Prejudice you will not be subjected to drawn-out discussions about Allah's Revelations.

I am not a religious scholar and I don't pretend to be. It would be the height of presumption on my part to think that I could properly mine the Koran for purported hidden meanings behind "Verses which are elaborately formulated and clearly expounded from the Wise, the All-Aware", to quote Allah. I prefer letting Allah and His Messenger, the Prophet Muhammad, speak for themselves, offering only a layman's opinion, or an expert's explanation, where I feel one is warranted. When Fakhry's crisp translation is not sufficient, it is Moududi I most often turn to.

Abul A'la Moududi's (also spelt Maududi) [1903-1979] credentials as a pre-eminent Islamic scholar are impeccable: journalist, theologian, Muslim revivalist, Islamist philosopher, first recipient of the *King Faisal International Award* for his services to Islam and Islamic studies. Of the more than 120 books he wrote, he is most famous for his magnum opus *The Meaning of the Qur'an*.

The Koran is the book upon which the Taliban, the Islamist fundamentalist movement which ruled most of Afghanistan from 1996 until 2001, based their concept of God's government on earth. The Taliban, like all believers, were, and are required to at least attempt to commit to memory the entire Koran. Believers are also expected to accept Allah's Revelations in their totality without question. This has not been my approach in presenting my impressions, the impressions of a former Catholic, now an agnostic, on first reading the Koran.

As an unbeliever, I hope I can safely express my opinions about the Koran and the Prophet Muhammad, although nothing is certain. It is an unfortunate fact of life that authors who choose to write about Islam, the Koran or the life of the Prophet Muhammad must tread carefully lest the believers perceive their writings as an insult to Islam. I hope that I have achieved that fine balance, if such an equilibrium is even possible.

Translations of the Koran are usually called interpretations because believers claim that only the Arabic version of the Koran can convey the true meaning of God's words. If you can't read the Koran in the original, they say, you are bound to misinterpret Allah's words. Do they have a point, or is it just a pre-emptive rationalisation? A pre-emptive excuse for some of the frightening revelations contained within the Muslim Holy Book. Revelations that may leave some unbelievers wondering if it is God's words they are reading or those of His nemesis?

The Koran is written in verses or ayats, therefore it is true that you will not be able to appreciate the rhythm and rhyme that only the original can convey, but any good translation will be able to communicate the meaning of the poet's words and the meaning of the words is what you should be concerned with.

An English translation of the Koran will run to about 77,700 words; the approximate size of a standard 300 page book. A book, Allah reveals, in which you can study "Whatever you choose."

68:35 Shall We consider those who submit like those who are criminals?

68:36 What is the matter with you; how do you judge?

68:37 Or do you have a Book in which you study?

68:38 Wherein there is whatever you choose.

It is a bold statement for a relatively small book where boundless repetitions use up print space that could, perhaps, be put to better use.

The Koran is made up of 114 chapters or surahs. When referring to chapters of the Koran, I use the Arabic transliteration (converting from one alphabet to another) of chapter, which is surah. Each surah is further divided into verses. I have chosen to remain with the English understanding of what is an ayat.

There are 6,346 verses in the Koran if you include the 112 unnumbered Basmalahs, the formula-invocation "in the name of Allah, the Compassionate, the Merciful" which appears at the beginning of every chapter of the Koran except the first and the ninth.

In *Pain, Pleasure and Prejudice* I refer to verses by the surah number and verse; for example, verse 2:282. Or by surah name and verse: *The Cow, verse* 282. A verse can be just a few words long or more than 200 words such as verse 2:282, the longest verse in the Koran which deals, in part, with the virtue of good bookkeeping practices and why, when it comes to transactions involving money or chattel, a woman on her own cannot be trusted to accurately remember things.

Towards the end of some chapters you will find supplementary material following a squiggly line (~~~). It is additional information which I consider important that could not be conveniently presented in footnotes.

Just a few editorial notes before we get down to business and let God speak for Himself. All quotes from the Koran are from Majid Fakhry's interpretation unless otherwise indicated. Text added by Fakhry within a quoted verse to improve understanding is enclosed within square "[ ]" brackets. Other clarifications by Fakhry, including footnotes, are enclosed in round "( )" brackets. On rare occasions, you will find italicised bracketed comments within a verse. These are the author's and are usually included to identify who Allah does not explicitly name where He reveals someone said this and that, and when it is not evident, to the casual reader, who He is instructing when He tells His Messenger what to say in response to questions and observations from person, or persons, to whom he is reciting Allah's revelations.

Any underlining of words in verses for emphasis is my doing not Fakhry's. I hope that Majid will forgive me if I have use in my writing the more familiar Koran instead of Qur'an as he does.

At the beginning of twenty surahs, following the invocation *In the Name of Allah the Compassionate, the Merciful*, are letters, or groups of letters of the alphabet e.g. Alif – Lam – Ra. According to some Islamic scholars, these letters are abbreviations or Muqatta'at, of Arabic words, in this instance, the English meaning can be interpreted as "I am Allah, the Most Seeing." Other Islamic scholars, according to Fakhry, believe they are "secret symbols with which the Angel Gabriel opened the revelation or surah in question." I have included these letters or groups of letters in quoted verses where they appear.

Where warranted, verses are accompanied by sayings or descriptions of actions of the Prophet called hadiths (Ahadith is often use to indicate the plural form, but not here). Hadiths, of which there are tens of thousands, are hearsay evidence collected approximately 200 years after the Prophet's passing of what God's Messenger said and did, including the silent approval of actions done in his presence. A authentic (sahih) or good (hasan) hadith i.e. one that can be traced to a witness of what the Prophet said or did, or did not do, via of chain of reliable transmitters, is usually considered a legal precedent if it does not contradict the Koran[1].

In at least 300 revelations, what Allah reveals of his Koran is in the form of telling His Messenger what to say in what are responses or appear to be responses to questions or observations from believers and unbelievers listening to the Prophet deliver the latest batch of revelations delivered by Allah's intermediary Messenger, the angel

---

[1] Sunni Islam considers the hadiths collected by six men ((al-Bukhari, Imam Muslim, At-Tirmidi, Ibn Majah, Abu Dawood and An-Nisa'i) with the al-Bukhari collection being the largest and considered the most authoritative as the "six canonical collections." Imam Bukhari (d. 870) is said to have gathered over 600,000 hadiths of which 7,275 are considered authentic. The Koran and these "hadith collections" inform every facet of a believer's existence.

Gabriel. When you encounter the word "say" followed by a colon in a revelation (with no other qualifier such as "they" e.g. "they say" or on a rare occasions "you said") unless otherwise indicated, you may assume it to be Allah telling His Messenger what to say.

One final editorial observation: all quoted verses have been carefully reviewed to ensure that Fakhry's interpretation has been faithfully rendered. Many verses such as 44:43-44 must be read together to form a complete sentence or thought; therefore do not assume a typographical (typo) or grammatical error if a verse does not end with the expected punctuation.

> 44:43 The Tree of Zaqqum (the Tree of Bitterness) will certainly be

> 44:44 The food of the sinner.

Finally, some of the quoted verses from Fakhry's interpretation of the Koran have no closing quotes and it has to do with an often misunderstood rule of English grammar. If the material being quoted is more than one paragraph .i.e. verses, you can get away with only opening quotation marks (") at the beginning of each verse and only supply closing quote (") at the end of the complete multiple paragraph quotation.

~~~~~~~~~~~~~~~~~~~

Is it a translation or an interpretation? Most translators of the Koran are careful to highlight, by enclosing in round or square brackets what is not in the original text, or when they offer an explanation of what is meant by this or that phrase. Fakhry is one of those, an exception being what Allah may have intended to say when He revealed that He had made the sun and the moon "subservient" to man.

> 14:33 And He has made subservient to you the sun and the moon pursuing their courses, and subjected also the night and the day.

Yusuf Ali's translation closely parallels Fakhry's, the main difference being "subjected to you" instead "subservient to you" and "also" is enclosed in quotes.

> 14:33 And He hath made subject to you the sun and the moon, both diligently pursuing their courses; and the night and the day hath he (also) made subject to you.

Muhammad Assad uses square brackets to show what he believes Allah means by "subservient".

> 14:33 And has made the sun and the moon, both of them constant upon their courses, subservient [to His laws, so that they be of use] to you; and has made the night and the day subservient [to His laws, so that they be of use] to you.

All three rendering of revelation 14:33 could be considered translations, but perhaps not a fourth by M. M. Pickthall, a Christian convert to Islam.

> 14:33 And maketh the sun and the moon, constant in their courses, to be of service unto you, and hath made of service unto you the night and the day.

All translations consulted in the extensive research for Pain, Pleasure and Prejudice are from recognized Islamic scholars of the Koran.

A Divine Bias

Sex as a Pavlovian Reaction

When Allah talks about sex, whether it is about sex between husband and wife or extra-marital sex (a form of sex that is only available to the husband) it is almost exclusively about sex as being a man's reward for being faithful to Allah. When you find women and sex mentioned in the same verse you will usually find Allah explaining how women are naturally drawn to men, that wanting to have sex with men is what they yearn for. This irrepressible longing to want to touch and be touched is why they must be restrained from their natural tendencies to want to seduce every man in sight and bring chaos to the orderly world of the Koran.

In the Koran, it is the females (married and unmarried, maid-servants, slaves-girls, post and pre-pubescent girls) who lust after the naked male body who are almost always the sexual aggressors. A female can also be expected to lie about a sexual assault, for example, falsely accusing a man of attempted rape when, in reality, she was the aggressor. From the story of Joseph in Egypt whose benefactor's wife would have him sleep with her, by force, if necessary:

> 12:25 They raced to the door, and she ripped his shirt from behind. When they met her husband at the door, she said: "What is the penalty of one who intended evil for your wife except imprisonment or severe punishment?"

Exceptionally, Allah, when recounting this encounter, acknowledges that men can, on rare occasions, be the aggressors and how you can tell.

> 12:26 He (Joseph) said: "She sought to seduce me." And a member of her household bore witness: "If his shirt was torn from the front, then she is telling the truth and he is a liar.

12:27 "But if his shirt is torn from behind, then she lies and he is one of the truthful."

While admitting that men can, on occasion, be forceful in the pursuit of intimacy, Allah makes another generalization about women ... *that they are skilled in the art of deception.* <u>Notice the plural form of woman,</u> "you women", in verse 12:28.

12:28 When he (the husband) saw that his shirt was torn from behind, he said: "This is part of your guile, you women. Your guile is indeed very great.

It is less clear in verse 12:29 whether Allah considers women, in general, as being sinners. The tone of the husband in admonishing his wife and the fact that he doesn't refer to her by name or her relationship to him e.g. "you, my wife", but as a member of a group would suggest a certain contempt for her sex; a contempt that a sinner might elicit from a god.

12:29 "Joseph, overlook this matter; and you woman, ask forgiveness for your sin. You are indeed one of the sinners."

When it comes to women and their sexual allure Allah doesn't give men much credit either. For Allah, the sight of a single strand of a woman's hair can cause a man to experience a Pavlovian-like reaction, an uncontrollable urge to hump the owner of the stray hair then and there.

Men, no matter what their marital status, must resist the advances of maid-servants, slaves and pre-pubescent girls (girls who have yet to begin menstruating, what most of us would call children) at least three times. If after being denied three times, the maid-servant, the slave or the pre-pubescent girl still insist on having a piece of you, Allah has decreed that resistance would be futile and permission is given for the man to have sex or indulge in sexual touching with the supplicant.

Fakhry, in a footnote, argues that "approach each other" in the following verse means that maid-servants, slaves and pre-pubescent girls are allowed "to attend to you." Since in the case of maid-servants and slaves that is part of their function, my interpretation would be that the man is allowed to have sex with them including sex with pre-pubescent girls. Whether its full-blown intercourse, or just sexual touching is another matter. Also, this is one of the few, if not the only time, that Fakhry translates what your "right hands possess" as slaves and not slave-girls, which could be significant.

> 24:58 O believers, let those your right hands possess (slaves and maid-servants) and those who have not reached the age of puberty ask your leave three times: (to attend to you or approach you) before the dawn prayer, when you put off your clothes at noon and after the evening prayer. These are three occasions of nudity for you; after which you are or they are not at fault, if you approach each other. That is how Allah makes clear His signs to you. Allah is All-Knowing, Wise.

Your children who have reached the age of puberty should also ask your permission to come into your presence in the three occasions described in 24:58.

> 24:59 And when your children reach puberty, let them ask leave, as those who came before them asked leave. That is how Allah makes clear His Signs to you. Allah is All-Knowing, Wise.

A man could be naked in front of his slave-girls, maids or pre-pubescent girls if the cause of his nakedness was because he was getting ready for prayer. What about around the house? Yes, if only his wives or slave-girls are present. Consider the following revelations on some of the qualities found in a believer:

THE BELIEVERS

23 Al-Mu'minûn

In the Name of Allah,
the Compassionate, the Merciful

23:1 The believers have prospered;

23:2 Those who are submissive in their prayers,

23:3 And those who turn away from idle talk,

23:4 And those who give the alms.

23:5 <u>And those who guard their private parts,</u>

23:6 Except from their wives and what their right hands possess (slave-girls). [For these] they are not blameworthy.

23:7 Whoever seeks anything beyond that – those are the transgressors.

If wives and what your "right hands possess", revelation 23:6, can manipulate your private parts for the purpose of bringing about your sexual release, can you do it yourself? No! Masturbation in Islam is a sin.

When Resistance is Futile

Women, like men, have been endowed by their creator with freewill[2] so how does a god ensure that men will get all the sex they desire in this world without taking away a woman's right to choose? What God giveth God can take away and Allah, in a god-like way, leaves instructions with His Messenger when it comes to women and sex that make it difficult, if not impossible for women to deny men their sexual favours.

Why would God have to do this if, as I claim, Allah believed women want to have sex all the time? Could Allah have been wrong in His assessment of women and instead of admitting that women are more complicated than He first imagined, piled on a whole and complicated set of rules that would ensure that His creation behaved the way He intended. In Allah's account of the creation of the first couple, the first man actually, Eve is barely mentioned, and not by name. In fact, when it comes to women and girls, the only female that He mentions by name in the entire Koran is Mary, mother of Jesus, and then mainly to emphasise that she was not the mother of a god.

Allah admits to putting some thought into Adam's creation, a creation He is extremely proud of and rightly so. Eve, however, appears to be an afterthought. She sort of appears out of the blue. Adam gets most of the attention anywhere the couple is mentioned including the following verses where we first meet the *first* couple. In these revelations, the proud Creator does not ask Satan to prostrate himself before the happy twosome, only before Adam. The only reference to Eve is in the second verse and even then Allah does not mention her by name, just as the wife of Adam.

---

[2] The concept of freewill or freedom to make your own choices is very narrowly defined in Islam. In practical terms, for believers, it means surrendering yourself to God or rejecting him. Once you have surrendered your "will" to God, your freewill is effectively extinguished. A verse to that effect:

31:22 Whoever surrenders his will to Allah while doing the right, has surely grasped the firmest handle. Unto Allah is the ultimate issue of all affairs.

2:34 And when We said to the angels; "Prostrate yourselves before Adam", they all prostrated themselves except Iblis (Satan), who refused, out of pride and was one of the disbelievers.

2:35 Then we said: "O Adam, dwell in Paradise, you and your wife, and eat from it as much as you wish and wherever you wish, but do not approach this tree (meaning to not eat from it) or you will be unjust.

Allah not only cast the first couple out of Paradise but on at least two occasions admits to having made them enemies of one another.

2:36 But Satan caused them to fall down from it and be turned out of the bliss they had been in. And We said: "Go down [from Paradise to earth] being enemies one to the other. And you will have in the earth an abode and sustenance for a while."

20:123 He (Allah) said: "Go down from it both of you, as enemies of one another; but should guidance from Me come to you, he who follows My Guidance will not go astray or suffer.

It is not clear if Allah ever forgave Eve for eating the fruit of the forbidden tree. If He did not, this would explain a great deal.

20:120 But the Devil whispered to him, saying "O Adam, shall I show you the Tree of Immortality and a kingdom which will never perish?"

20:121 And so they both (Adam and Eve) ate from it; whereupon their shameful parts were revealed to them and they started fastening upon themselves leaves of Paradise. Adam thus disobeyed his Lord and so went astray.

20:122 Then, his Lord favoured him, and so he relented towards him, and guided him.

2:37 Then Adam received words from his Lord, Who forgave him. He is indeed the All-Forgiving, the Merciful.

Could a male god[3] who shuns female companionship and is obviously enamoured with the male half of humankind be expected to know anything significant about the other half? Would any woman feel comfortable with such a god telling her what to do, what to wear, what men expect of her? Would most women fear that such a god would harbour the same prejudices and insecurities as normal men when it comes to dealing with her sex? Would a god that understood women leave instructions that will make it difficult, if not impossible, for any believing woman to deny her husband her body under almost any circumstances? Would a god that understood women leave the impression that they crave sex all the time, and will have sex with any man, anywhere, any time?

If women are just one big, yearning sexual machine, then Allah is indeed All-Knowing. If they are more than that, then Allah is all wet and the God of the Koran doesn't know women at all and His advice to women is suspect. Being preoccupied with sex and knowing anything about sex are two different things – just ask the Pope.

Sex for Allah, as mentioned previously, is a means to an end. It is a way of gaining and rewarding the loyalty of men. Having come to the conclusion that men aspire to no higher ideals than to fornicate to their hearts content, He promises them sex in spades in this world and even more in the next if they will worship Him and only Him. Women's loyalty, on the other hand, will be assured by making men their overlords and in the process provide loyal, believing men with plenty of earth-bound sex while awaiting even more abundant sex in heaven.

Why Muslim Men Are Always Right

Men will be men and gods will be gods and both will show a bias towards their sex when dealing with the opposite sex. The Greeks and Romans probably meant to reduce this divine bias by creating goddesses; Indians by creating gods that combined both male and female attributes. Even pre-Islamic Arabs worshipped goddesses, the most famous being al-Lat, al-Uzza and Manat. Depending on what favour you wanted granted, you prayed to a god or a goddess. For example, you prayed to the fertility goddess Al-Lat for obvious reasons.

---

[3] Islamic scholars have argued that Allah is a sexless being and has no gender. The use of the pronoun"He" is made necessary when referring to Allah in the third person because Arabic has no word for "it".

Allah and His Messenger changed all that. Why? Why did they create what some would call "the men's religion", a religion that objectifies women and gives men ownership rights? Allah, you could say, was a "real man's" god. A God who went out of His way to make sure believing men were sexually satisfied, and for most men that is a good thing. Many believing women seem to be satisfied with this arrangement as well.

Why would what appears to be a majority of believing women be satisfied with a god giving men complete control over their sexual, home and public life, including denying them the right <u>not</u> to have children or to refuse to have sex whether it be for pleasure or procreation? Is it the Stockholm syndrome on steroids? The believing woman having been a prisoner for so long learns to cherish her captivity, her divinely appointed male guardian and to fear the words of a vengeful God who says that is the way it must be lest she spend an eternity burning in Hell.

Many questions remain. Did the Prophet Muhammad feel threatened by women? Does Allah feel threatened by women? Was the Prophet looking to Allah for more than help with his love life? Did God's Messenger nurture some deep-seated resentment against women? Did Allah or His Messenger believe that pre-Islamic women were becoming too full-of-themselves, too independent and had to be brought down a peg or two – to be put in their place?

The Prophet Muhammad owed his success as a merchant to an older woman who hired the good-looking, allegedly illiterate young man to lead her caravans and later bankrolled his operations. Did he resent the fact that it was a woman that helped him get started and who probably kept him in business and later spent her wealth in support of his ministry? It was this same successful businesswoman, now his wife, who re-assured her husband that it was God talking to him, not Satan or some other godless creature when her husband began having visions. This was before the Prophet was made aware that the devil usually took the female form.

> Jabir reported that Allah's Messenger (may peace be upon him) saw a woman, and so he came to his wife, Zaynab, as she was tanning a leather and had sexual intercourse with her. He then went to his Companions and told them: The woman advances and retires in the shape of a devil, so when one of you sees a woman, he should come to his wife, for that will repel what he feels in his heart. *Sahih Muslim*

Gheorghiu tells the touching story of how, when the Prophet Muhammad had a vision in his home and was unsure if it was Satan or an angel, his wife Khadijah proved to her husband that it was an angel. She told her husband to get undressed and she did the same and they embraced. Do you still see him, she asked? No, said God's Messenger! Then it must have been an angel, she said, because an angel would not have remained to stare at a naked couple embracing.

Why would a man who had married such a bright, successful woman as Khadijah, the woman to whose intelligence, financial and moral support he owed much of his success accept Allah's conclusion that women were not as smart as men; that women had trouble doing simple arithmetic and had poor memories. Why did Khadijah's husband not at least argue with Allah, when he received the following revelation, that, based on his experience with Khadijah, women were not dummies; revelation 2:282, among other things, instructs the believer as to how many people are required to witness the contracting of a debt by a mentally or physically handicapped person.

> 2:282 O believers, when you contract a debt for a fixed period, write it down. Let a scribe write it for you with fairness. No scribe should decline to write as Allah has taught him. So let him then write and let the debtor dictate. He should fear his Lord and not diminish the debt in the least. If the debtor is feeble-minded or week or ignorant, then let his guardian dictate with fairness. <u>And call to witness two witnesses of your men; if not two men, then one man and two women from such witnesses you approve of, so that if one of them (the two women) fails to remember, the other will remind her.</u> The witnesses should not decline [to testify] when they are called upon [to do so]. So do not be averse to writing down the debt, be it small or large, as well as when it is due. This is more equitable in Allah's sight; more suitable for testimony and less likely to rouse your doubts. If it is an instant transaction among yourselves (involving no debt); then it is no offence if you do not write it down. And let there be witnesses when you sell one to another; but neither the scribe nor the witness should be harmed, because if you do that, it is an act of transgression. Fear Allah; Allah teaches you. He has knowledge of everything.

If revelation 2:282 had been interpreted as Allah stating that women were not good at business this would have been the lesser of two evils. Unfortunately, it has been interpreted as meaning that women require more witnesses in different court proceedings that have nothing to do with commercial or financial transactions, such as accusations of adultery or sexual assault.

Allah is not satisfied with just claiming that women are bad at math and can't remember things as well as men. For Allah, men are superior to women in everything by at least one degree – whatever a degree is. He reminds the believers of this rule in a verse where He instructs women on how long they must wait after divorce before being seen in the company of men and what the divorcing couple can or cannot do during this waiting period.

> 2:228 Divorced women should keep away from men for three menstrual periods. And it is not lawful for them to conceal that which Allah has created in their wombs, if they truly believe in Allah and the Last Day. Their husbands have the right in the meantime to take them back, should they seek reconciliation; and women have rights equal to what is incumbent upon them according to what is just, although men are one degree above them (what is meant here is that the men have a superior authority). Allah is Mighty, Wise.

Verse 2:228 can also be interpreted as Allah saying that if there is any disagreement about anything I have said, the man's point of view shall prevail, or that a man's word is worth more than a woman's. Islamic laws and traditions hold both interpretations to be true.

~~~~~~~~~~~~~~~

On the road and no bookkeeper can be found:

> 2:282 O believers, when you contract a debt for a fixed period, write it down. Let a scribe write it for you with fairness. No scribe should decline to write as Allah has taught him …

> 2:283 If you are travelling and cannot find a scribe, a security should be taken. But if you trust one another, then let him who is entrusted deliver the security and fear Allah his Lord. Do not withhold the testimony. He who withholds it has a sinful heart. Allah has knowledge of what you do.

2:284 To Allah belongs whatever in the heavens and on earth. And whether you reveal or conceal what is in your hearts, Allah will call you to account for it. He will then forgive whom He wills, and punish whom He wills. He is Able to do everything.

A Prophet and Prude

A Western reader of the Koran and the sayings of the Prophet Muhammad is struck by the male-centric universe that Allah and His Messenger expound and praise, and the low esteem in which both hold females, especially God's Messenger:

> Narrated 'Aisha: "The things which annul the prayers were mentioned before me. They said, Prayer is annulled by a dog, a donkey and a woman (if they pass in front of the praying people)..." *Bukhari*

> A'isha said [to Muhammad]: "You have made us equal to the dogs and the asses." *Muslim*

> Treat women well, for they are like domestic animals (awan) with you and do not possess anything for themselves. *Tabari vol.9 p.113*

> The Prophet said, "Isn't the witness of a woman equal half that of a man?" The women said, "Yes." He said: "This is because of the deficiency of the woman's mind." *Bukhari*

While Allah created a religion that promises men just about all the sex they can handle in this world and even more sex in the Hereafter, His Messenger is still a bit of a prude when it comes to sex. Gheorghiu tells the story of how when the Prophet Muhammad first arrived in Medina and discovered that date bearing palms were artificially pollinated he was scandalized and ordered the practice stopped. He re-instituted the practice the next year after date production plummeted, but insisted it be done when he wasn't around.

Considering that the Prophet was officially married to fourteen women, kept a number of concubines for company and an unknown number of slave-girls, his extraordinary prudishness is surprising, to say the least. Prudish men are known to be both attracted and repelled by the sex act, a trait often shared with misogynous males. For both stereotypes, a woman is both an object of desire and of contempt. The kind of contempt clearly evident in the following hadiths where God's Messenger fixes the distance, if there is no physical barrier, that women, Jews, dogs, pigs and donkeys must maintain from a praying Muslim male.

> Ikrimah reported on the authority of Ibn Abbas, saying: "I think the Apostle of Allah said: 'When one of you prays without a sutrah (a barrier), a dog, an ass, a pig, a Jew, a Magian, and a woman cut off his prayer, but it will suffice if they pass in front of him at a distance of over a stone's throw.'" *Abu Dawud*

Could this prudish middle-aged man's struggle between contempt and desire for the dozens of mostly young females he secluded within his household be responsible for the double standard in Islamic law and the disdain for females evident in many of Allah's revelations. Did contempt win out, which is why believing women are in class by themselves, the lowest class.

~~~~~~~~~~~~~~~~

Allah does not engage in sex. If sex is beneath Him (no pun intended) the Prophet's prudishness may also have something to do with protecting Allah from being exposed to the sex act or the end-result of sexual activity, even of the unintentional kind i.e. nocturnal emissions (no quotation marks were in the original translation and I have chosen not to add any).

> Narrated Aisha, Ummul Mu'minin: The Prophet (peace be upon him) was asked about a person who found moisture (on his body or clothes) but did not remember the sexual dream. He replied: He should take a bath. He was asked about a person who remembered that he had a sexual dream but did not find moisture. He replied: Bath is not necessary for him. Umm Salamah then asked: Is washing necessary for a woman if she sees that (in her dream)? He replied: Yes. Woman are counterpart of men. *Abu Dawud, Book #1, Hadith #0236*

And then, there is his demand that the entrance to houses not face the mosque because the mosque is not lawful "for a menstruating woman and for a person who is sexually defiled".

> Narrated Aisha, Ummul Mu'minin: The Apostle of Allah (peace be upon him) came and saw that the doors of the

houses of his Companions were facing the mosque. He said: Turn the direction of the houses from the mosque. The Prophet (peace be upon him) then entered (the houses or the mosque), and the people did take any step in this regard hoping that some concession might be revealed. He the Prophet) again came upon them and said: Turn the direction of these (doors) from the mosque I do not make the mosque lawful for a menstruating woman and for a person who is sexually defiled. *Abu Dawud, Book #1, Hadith Book #1, Hadith #0232*

Who Gets What

Which came first: the divine instructions that led to the seclusion of believing women or the divine instructions that made it easier for men to accumulate wealth at the expense of believing women? An argument could be made that the first made the second inevitable.

The Invisible, Illiterate Woman

Allah's instructions on how women should dress, with whom they can be seen in public and how they should behave in private and in public have been interpreted in traditional Islamic societies as meaning that women should be invisible except to their immediate family, their husbands and, with certain restrictions, their husband's family. A good believing wife will not invite into her husband's home anyone of either sex whom he does not approve of.

In keeping with Allah's commands, traditional Islamic societies require that post-pubescent girls (teenagers) and women remain secluded in their fathers' or husbands' houses. If they must go out in public they are required to be accompanied by their father, husband or a male relative covered from head-to-toe in a voluminous sack-like blue garment with a mesh grid over the eyes (a burqua) or a shapeless black robe and black gloves with a face-covering black veil with a slit for the eyes (a niqab)[4].

Traditional Islamic societies guided by Allah's ideal of the perfect women, see the post-pubescent female's role in simple terms: baby making machines, stay-at-home mothers, housekeepers and sexual gratification objects. Daughters are married off as early as possible after they have started menstruating and in some countries even earlier, as in Iran for example.

The Ayatollah Khomeini in his monumental collection of commentaries on Islamic jurisprudence and morality, the

---

[4] Usually a sign that the individual is a follower of one of the stricter and more radical schools of Sunni Islam.

Tahrirolvasyleh, wrote that "it was better in the eyes of God if a girl started menstruating in the home of her husband instead of that of her father and that any father marrying his daughter so young will have a permanent place in heaven."

In traditional Islamic households the mother is expected to raise her daughters until her husband can arrange an advantageous and usually profitable marriage. A marriage to a relative is preferred, usually an uncle or a nephew so as to keep the wealth within the clan, tribe or family and to strengthen clan, tribal and familial ties. The mother is also responsible for raising sons until they reach the age of seven, when the proud father will then take over their up-bringing.

Considering the onerous restrictions placed on women in traditional Islamic societies and their limited role in their children's education which consists mostly of teaching them the Koran and familiarizing them with Islamic laws and traditions it is understandable, only reasonable, that higher education for women and girls would be seen as a luxury by many in the umma, the community of believers. The Taliban took the interpretation of the Koranic view of believing women's limited but crucial role as mothers, housekeepers and lovers to its logical extreme and simply denied females the right to a formal education.

The severe dress code, the denial of an education at least equal to a man's and the restrictions placed on women's freedom of movement in traditional Islamic societies makes it extremely difficult, if not impossible, for women to work in a well-remunerated job outside the home or in a job that will earn them as much as a man. Also, the lion's share of any wealth they may accumulate must, under Allah's inheritance and property laws, sooner or later, usually sooner, end up in the pockets of their husband, their husband's brothers, their husband's parents and their male offsprings. The net result is that, in traditional Islamic societies, it is next to impossible for women to earn an income of their own or accumulate any real wealth, thus making them totally subservient and beholden to the men who have the means of providing them with everything from the basic necessities of life to simple luxuries.

I suspect that the Prophet's first wife, an independent, wealthy woman in her own right, would not have been pleased. The Prophet, we are told, loved and respected his first wife, which is why I believe the forced seclusion of women and all the ills that it entails may have had nothing to do with Allah wishing to condemn believing women to a prisoner-like, subsistence existence. This forced seclusion of women and teenaged girls may just have been Allah's way of helping His middle-aged Messenger manage his burgeoning household of beautiful young wives, concubines and slave-girls. Some of His revelations pertaining to the close supervision of females may also have been meant to ensure that His Messenger was never again embarrassed by the type of rumours that circulated when the youngest of his fourteen wives, Aisha, got lost in the desert and was found and returned to the Prophet the next day by a young man, and to stop his women from gossiping about what went on behind closed doors.

While the seclusion of women may have been an unintentional consequence of the Allah trying to help His Messenger, He did close a number of loopholes in pre-Islamic laws and traditions that might lead women to "accidentally" accumulate wealth or at least more wealth than a man; for example, inherited wealth. To avoid such an eventuality God's Messenger received a number of revelations on the disposition of an inheritance from a deceased spouse.

Wills and Witnesses

> 5:106 O believers, when death approaches any of you, let two just men from among you act as witnesses at the time of testament; or two other from another folk if you happen to be travelling abroad and are overtaken by the calamity of death. You will detain them (the two others) after the prayer and they will swear by Allah if you are in doubt: "We will not sell Him [Allah] for any price, even if a near kinsman is involved and we will not keep secret the Testimony of Allah (the testimony which Allah enjoins); for then we would surely be sinners."

On first reading of revelation 5:106 it would appear that only men can bear witness to a will. Allah's inclusion of "another folk" may have given Islamic scholar a way of allowing women to bear witness to a will without running afoul of Allah's men-only decree.

The legal requirements for the validation of wills will vary from country to country where the requirements of Islamic law are not recognized as legally binding. Where Islamic law or the Sharia is permitted, or is the law of the land, an attempt must usually be made to find two believing men to witness a will. If two male believers cannot be found to witness a will, one or two male non-believers may be asked to perform the duties of the believers. If no males, or only one male can be found, then up to four females may be called upon as witness in keeping with Allah's observation in revelation 2:282 about women being unreliable witnesses: "… And call to witness two witnesses of your men; if not two men, then one man and two women from such witnesses you approve of, so that if one of them (the two women) fails to remember, the other will remind her…" The witnesses should, of course, be sinless and swear to that effect.

> 5:107 If, however, it is discovered that they have committed a sin, then two others shall take their places from among those against whom the first two had sinned. Whereupon they shall swear by Allah: "Our testimony is more truthful than their testimony and we have not transgressed, or else we would surely be evildoers."

> 5:108 Thus, it is likelier that they will bear witness properly, or fear that other oaths will contradict their own oaths. Fear Allah and listen well; for Allah does not guide the wicked people.

Another revelation about what to do when death approaches which, "According to some classical commentators", writes Fakhry in a footnote, "… was abrogated by the law of inheritance."

> 2:180 It is prescribed for you that when death is imminent for one of you and he leaves wealth, he should equitably make a testament in favour of the parents and the near of kin. This in incumbent upon the righteous.

A self-evident revelation about whoever falsifies a will, followed by what should be an equally manifest revelation, that helping a dying man and his kin come to an understanding as to the fair dispossession of his estate is not a sin.

> 2:181 Whoever then changes it after he had heard it, the sin committed is that of those who change it. Allah is All-Hearing, All-Knowing.

> 2:182 Should anyone, however, fear any inequity or offence from a testator and reconciles them (the testator and the beneficiary), he shall incur no sin. Allah is Forgiving, Merciful.

Husband Dies

Following are revelations pertaining to the disposition of a recently deceased male's property. As mentioned earlier, male offsprings get the lion's share. Sisters are only entitled to half the share of a brother and, if there are more than two females, the male is entitled to one-third, with the rest being divided among the females (I assume sisters) whatever their number.

> 4:11 Allah commands you, with respect to your children, that the male shall inherit the equivalent of the share of two females. If there be more than two females, then they should receive two-thirds of what he (the deceased father) leaves; but if there is only one female, she is entitled to one-half …

If he did not father any children and he has no brothers:

> 4:11 … To each of his parents, one-sixth of what he leaves, if he has any children; but if he has no children, then his parents will inherit him, the mother receiving one third …

If he has any brothers and dies childless the formula changes. No mention is made of sisters of the deceased being entitled to anything in this revelation.

> 4:11 … But if he has any brothers[5], then his mother receives one-sixth, after any will he had made or any debt he had incurred [is taken care of] …

The verse ends with Allah acknowledging that it is difficult to choose between who is the better investment, fathers or sons (no mention is made of daughters or mothers) when it comes to the proceeds of an inheritance and finishes with the usual praise for the rule maker.

> 4:11 … Your fathers and sons – you know not who of them is of greater advantage to you. This is a law from Allah; Allah surely is All-Knowing, Forbearing.

Less they missed it the first time; Allah reminds the believers of His two-for-one rule in His instructions on the disposition of an

---

[5] Proving that even rulings from Allah can be interpreted so as to increase their equitability, brothers of the deceased father in the Shi'ite version of Islam are not automatically entitled to a share of an inheritance.

inheritance where the only beneficiaries are brothers and sisters of the deceased.

> 4:176 [If] they consult you, say: "Allah enjoins you regarding him who dies leaving neither children nor parents. If he leaves a sister; she is entitled to half of what he leaves behind; and he inherits her if she has no children. If he leaves two sisters, they are entitled to two-thirds of what he leaves behind; but if they are brothers and sisters the male will have the equivalent of the share of two females. Allah makes it clear to you lest you go astray. Allah has full knowledge of everything!"

What about the family home? From my reading of the following revelation, the former wives of the dearly departed are allowed to stay in the family home for up to a year before the relatives of the deceased husband move in and they have to move out.

> 2:240 Those of you who die leaving wives behind should bequeath to them a year's provision without turning [them] out (from their homes). If however, they leave [their homes], then you (the relatives of the dead) incur no offence for what they do in a rightful way to themselves. Allah is Mighty, Wise.

Wife Dies

Allah's instructions as to the dispositions of a deceased wife's property, as far as I can tell, are all contained in verse 4:12. The key provision here again is that the husband who has lost his wife is entitled to more than a wife who has lost her husband,. The two-for-one rule appears to still apply. I will let you do the math.

> 4:12 You are entitled to half of what your wives leave, if they have no children; but if they have any children, then you are entitled to one-quarter of what they leave, after any will they had made or any loan they had incurred [is taken care of]. And they are entitled to one-quarter of what you leave, if you have no children; but if you have any children, then they are entitled to one-eighth of what you leave, after any will you had made or loan you had incurred [is taken care of]. And if a man or a woman dies having no children or parents, but has a brother or sister, then each shall have

one-sixth; if they are more than that, then they shall share one-third, after any will made or debt incurred [is taken care of] without prejudice. This is a Commandment from Allah, and Allah is All-Knowing, Forbearing.

Islamic scholars like Yahiya Emerick dismiss this double standard by saying "in Islam only the man is compelled to spend money in support of his family therefore he should be entitled to a bigger share of the inheritance." How convenient. *A woman, under a system that has made her less wealthy than her partner is denied her fair share because she is less wealthy than her partner.* Divine circular reasoning! Accept this decreed biased distribution of inherited wealth and you will be amply rewarded in the hereafter; don't, and the Fire will be waiting.

> 4:13 These are the Ordinances from Allah, and whoever obeys Allah and His Messenger, He will admit into Gardens beneath which rivers flow, abiding therein forever. That is the great victory!

> 4:14 But whoever disobeys Allah and His Messenger and transgresses His bounds, He will admit into the Fire, wherein he shall abide forever, and his will be a demeaning punishment.

Since Allah's Ordinances pertaining to wills overwhelmingly favour males, they are unlikely to transgress, therefore, the promise of eternal pain is probably meant for females who would seek a more equitable share. Remember, the pronouns he or him, usually refer to either or both sexes.

~~~~~~~~~~~~~~

Polygamous marriages must make determining a fair share for each wife from the 25% (or the 12.5% if children are involved) of their husband's estate somewhat difficult to determine. How do you arrive at a fair share for a young wife who has only been with her husband a short time, and another who has given him children and who, because of her age and other factors is unlikely to find another man to look after her.

The formula, even if Allah had decided to include one in His Koran and hastened the discovery of algebra to allow for unknown values such as the number of wives, days of marital bliss, pregnancies etc. would have been complicated in the extreme, and not befitting a god who likes to keep it simple e.g. his two for one rule.

A Vicious Circle

Allah's revelations as to the disposition of an inheritance are, in my opinion, part of a vicious circle of self-serving regulations that favour men and that ensure that Muslim women will always have difficulty accumulating the resources needed to look after themselves. Should they succeed in accumulating any wealth, on their death the lion's share of any wealth they might have inadvertently accumulated must go, by an order from God, to the male members of her husband's family and their male offsprings – their daughters, and their daughter's daughters... doomed in perpetuity to start their adult life at a disadvantage.

It is a vicious circle that ensures wealth, and the power it conveys, will invariably accumulate in the pockets of men. And what can a Muslim man do with the wealth so generously provided by Allah? Purchase the object of his affection. The woman or the girl dares not oppose the transaction; her very survival depending on the buyer's beneficence, Allah having denied her the means to look after herself.

Consider revelation 4:24 which makes it legal for believing men to use their wealth to purchase the females they intend to marry, as long as they are not on Allah's prohibited list, revelation 4:23. Verse 4:24, in addition to encouraging men to use their wealth to purchase wives, also makes it legal for them to marry the wives of another man if they have taken them as captives "Or married women except those your right hands possess (slave-girls)".

> 4:23 Unlawful to you are your mothers, your daughters, your sisters, your paternal and maternal aunts, your brother's daughters and sister's daughters, your foster-mothers who gave you suck, your foster-sisters, your wives' mothers, your step-daughters who are in your custody, born to your wives whom you have lain with. But if you have not lain with them then, then you are not at fault. [It is also not lawful to marry] the wives of your sons who are of your loins, or to take in two sisters together, unless this has already happened. Allah is truly All-Forgiving and Merciful!

> 4:24 Or married women except those your right hands possess (slave-girls). This is Allah's decree for you. <u>Beyond these it is lawful for you to seek, by means of your wealth,</u>

any women to marry and not to debauch. Those of them you have enjoyed, you should give them their dowry as a matter of obligation; but you are not liable to reproach for whatever you mutually agree upon, apart from the obligatory payment (the dowry). Allah is indeed All-Knowing, Wise.[6]

With the purchase came some responsibility: the responsibility to pay, to paraphrase Allah, the room and board for their wives, sons and daughters. In most societies, and Islamic society is no different, who pays the piper calls the tune – who pays the piper is in charge.

4:34 Men are in charge of women, because Allah has made some of them excel the others, and because they spend some of their wealth. Hence righteous women are obedient, guarding the unseen which Allah has guarded. And those of them that you fear might rebel, admonish them and abandon them in their beds and beat them. Should they obey you, do not seek a way of harming them; for Allah is Sublime and Great!

It really is a clever set-up worthy of a god. Making women dependent and beholden to the very men who, because of a divine ordinance, have legally deprived them of what was rightfully theirs and which would have given them the freedom to make their own choices on how they wished to live their lives.

~~~~~~~~~~~~~~~

Allah's Revelations pertaining to bequests from deceased parents or dead relatives. Details as to who gets what are not available.

4:7 Men should have a share of what parents and kinsmen leave behind; and women a share of what parents and kinsmen leave, whether big or small, as an obligatory portion.

4:8 And if the division is attended by kinsmen, orphans or poor men, then give them a share of it and speak to them kindly.

---

[6] Shi'ites have interpreted "you are not liable to reproach for whatever you mutually agree upon" to allow for temporary marriages. This is why young people in Iran can experiment with sex before entering into a "permanent" marriage without the female in the relationship risking being hanged or stoned to death for having sex outside marriage.

4:33 To every one We have appointed heirs to inherit part of what the parents or the kinsmen bequeath. Those with whom you made a compact, give them their share. Surely Allah is witness to everything.

~~~~~~~~~~~~~~

Allah said you should be kind to your slave-girls, but this kindness must not extend to sharing with them the extra that Allah may have given you, revelation 16:71. This may explain why there are no revelations about slave-girls being entitled to anything upon the death of their owners.

4:36 Worship Allah and do not associate with Him anything. Show kindness to the parents, to kinsmen, to orphans, the destitute, the close and distant neighbour, the companion by your side and those whom your right-hands possess. Allah does not love the arrogant and the boastful,

4:37 Those who are niggardly, and order other people to be niggardly, and conceal what Allah has given them of His Bounty, We have prepared for the unbelievers a demeaning punishment.

16:71 Allah has favoured some of you over others in provision; but those favoured will not give their provision to those whom their right hands possess so as to be equal therein. Will they then deny Allah's blessings?

It Is God's Will

Allah made women into a commodity that could be bartered and bargained for, befitting a god that selected a merchant as His Messenger. He also encouraged the accumulation of wealth in the pursuit of that commodity and made women beholden to the men who spent part of their wealth on their acquisition and for the continued provision of their basic necessities of life.

Women as a Field to Be Ploughed

How were women expected to repay the generous men who put food on their table, a roof over their heads and protected them from other men? Sex comes to mind. Beholden women will not necessarily see providing sex as payment for their room and board as the appropriate thing to do. Anyone who has ever paid a restaurant bill in the hope that sex will follow will understand this. For Allah, this ungrateful attitude was unacceptable. Not only that, a man might decide to take what he felt was his due, what he thought he had bought and paid for, and be punished for rape under pre-Islamic laws and traditions. To perhaps avoid a man being accused of raping his wife if she declined his request for intimacy, God's Messenger announced that he had received a revelation from Allah informing him that women had no right to refuse sex.

> 2:223 Your women are a tillage for you. So get to your tillage whenever you like. Do good for yourselves, fear Allah and know that you shall meet Him. And give good news to the believers.

It was good for you but was it good for her? Women as a field to be ploughed!!! What if the field is busy making dinner?

> Ali reported God's messenger as saying, "When a man calls his wife to satisfy his desire she must go to him even if she is occupied at the oven." *Tirmidhi*

What if the field doesn't want to be ploughed? What if the field has a headache? For the answer to this question, we must return to an already quoted verse, paying particular attention to when a wife is deserving of a beating.

> 4:34 ... And those of them that you fear might rebel, admonish them and abandon them in their beds and beat them. Should they obey you, do not seek a way of harming them; for Allah is Sublime and Great!

If a beating doesn't get her to change her mind and consent to sexual intercourse, then Allah will send an angel to try to convince her. At least, that is the Prophet's explanation.

> "if a husband invites his wife to have intimate relations with him, but the wife rejects him and he becomes angry all night long – for this his wife will be cursed by an angel until morning."[7]

Being cursed by an angel (the equivalent of being cursed by Allah) is not a trivial matter, as you may now appreciate.

Islamic scholars and learned clerics have long struggled with how much of a beating a wife should be forced to endure, and whether the Koran allows for the use of implements in the beating of one's spouse. According to God's Messenger, the beating should not be severe and yes, implements are allowed but should not be bigger than a toothbrush. The Prophet was said to be brushing his teeth when he answered this question. The toothbrush in question was probably some kind of reed, therefore a small whip would probably be allowed.

Leather merchants in Kabul did a brisk business in near meter long studded leather straps when the Taliban (Students of the Koran) were in power. As madrassa (Islamic schools) students, having spent most of their lives memorizing the Koran to the exclusion of any other type of learning, they may be excused for not being aware of the Prophet's advice on the size of the implement used to beat your wife.

---

[7] "With reference to this hadith, the majority of Islamic teachers say that it is sahih (proper, correct and valid)... including Bukhari [renowned collector of hadiths]... But within the Bukhari narrative, he does not express the sentence 'the husband becomes angry all night long'. While in other hadith narratives this sentence is considered the most important clause." *Rahima Online, Centre for Education on Islam and Women's Rights Issues.*

Women of the Book and Slave-Girls

Muslim women are not allowed to marry outside the faith but Muslim men are allowed to do so, as long as they marry Women of the Book – Jews, Christians and members of a religious sect called Sabians[8].

> 5:5 This day the good things have been made lawful to you; the food of the People of the Book is lawful to you, and your food is lawful to them; and so are the believing women who are chaste, and the chaste women of those who were given the Book before you, provided you give them their dowries and take them in marriage, not in fornication or as mistresses. If any one denies the faith, his work shall be of no avail to him, and in the Hereafter he will rank with the losers.

As you can appreciate, this last revelation expanded many-folds the available stock of virgins that a believing man could choose from. And if this still was not enough to satisfy your sexual appetite, or discriminating taste, or you could not afford a believing woman, you could always take wives from among your believing slave-girls.

> 4:25 Whoever of you cannot afford to marry a free, believing woman, let him choose from whatever your right hands possess (captives of war or slave-girls) of believing girls. Allah knows best your faith; you come one from the other. So marry them with their parents' leave and give them their dowry honourably, as chaste women, neither committing adultery nor taking lovers …

The pain a former slave-girl can expect if she cheats on her husband with another man, must take into account her previous status as a man's right hand possession.

> 4:25 … If they are legally married and commit adultery, their punishment shall be half that of a free women. Such is the law for those of you who fear committing sin; but to abstain is better for you. Allah is All-Forgiving and Merciful!

---

[8] "The Sabians were a Middle Eastern monotheistic religious group who worshipped in the names of stellar angels. Most of what is known of them comes from the Jewish philosopher Moses Maimonides [1135:1204] and classical Arabic sources." (Wiki).

Why all the rules about the women and girls a man can marry? It's a question of lust and Allah's Mercy.

> 4:26 Allah wants to explain to you [His laws] and to guide you along the paths of those who preceded you, and to be Merciful to you. Allah is All-Knowing, and Wise!

> 4:27 Allah also wants to be Merciful to you, but those who follow their lust want you to deviate greatly from the right course.

Some must have found revelation 4:27 somewhat amusing coming from a man with a penchant for beautiful girls as young as nine years old e.g. Aisha, with fourteen official wives, one of which was previously married to his adopted son Zayd but who he just had to have after seeing her almost naked, and an undisclosed number of concubines and slaves girls.

> 4:28 Allah wishes to lighten your burden; for man was created weak.

Marriage

Believers do not usually marry for love. Men acquire wives and, during the Prophet's time and the subsequent wars to expand Allah's Dominion, sex-slaves, what Allah refers to as "what your right hands possess", like you would acquire any property. Unlike most religions, a marriage in Islam is not a sacrament but a contract. A contract usually between members of the same clan, meaning you are all relatives, all offsprings of the same father a few generations removed. The marriage is usually an arranged affair and, not unlike arranged marriages of the Middle and Dark Ages, the primary consideration is what benefits in wealth and influence will accrue to the contracting parties i.e. the families of the bride and groom.

While marriage within the clan is encouraged, there are limits as to which relative or family member you can marry. Allah outlines these limits with His usual attention to detail in revelation 4:23, quoted earlier. And for a reason that again has nothing to do with the dangers of in-breeding[9], you should not marry a woman who was previously married to your father.

---

[9] The knowledge of the risk of reduced mental acuity and increased physical abnormalities due to inbreeding has not stop marriages between close relations in traditional Muslim societies such as Saudi Arabia. "In some parts of Saudi Arabia,

4:22 And do not marry women that your fathers had married, unless it has already happened. Surely it is indecent and hateful, and is an evil course!

If a man is unhappy with any of his matrimonial choices, getting out of a marriage agreement under Islamic law is probably easier than any other type of contractual arrangements. A marriage contract, unlike other contractual arrangements, is a one-sided affair, which can be terminated at the discretion of the male signatory. The soon-to-be-divorced wife cannot object to the unilateral breaking of the marriage contract by her husband.

Widows

Widows must wait four months and ten days before seeking a replacement for a deceased spouse. During this time they must not be seen in the company of men and must refrain from doing anything that would attract the attention of eligible suitors.

2:234 As for those of you who die leaving wives behind, their wives should observe a waiting period (during this period they should stay away from men) of four months and ten days. When they have completed that period you incur no offence on account of what they may do to themselves (such as adorning themselves or looking out for suitors) in a lawful manner. Allah has knowledge of what you do.

A man may, however, communicate to a widow, during the waiting period, his interest in making her his wife.

2:235 You incur no offence by disclosing your marriage proposals to women or by concealing them; Allah knows that you will remember them. And do not arrange anything secretly with them unless you speak what is recognized as true; and do not resolve on contracting the marriage until the prescribed period (the waiting period) ends. And know that Allah knows what you have in mind, and that Allah is Forgiving, Clement.

---

particularly in the south ... the rate of marriage among blood relatives ranges from 55 to 70 percent ... according to the Saudi government. Widespread inbreeding in Saudi Arabia has produced several genetic disorders Saudi public health officials said ... (New York Times, *Saudi Arabia Awakes to the Perils of Inbreeding*, May 1, 2003)"

Can a man obtain a window as an inheritance?

> 4:19 O believers, it is not lawful for you to inherit the women [of deceased kinsmen] against their will; nor restrain them in order to take away part of what you had given them, unless they commit flagrant adultery. Associate with them kindly; and if you feel aversion towards them, it may well be that you will be averse to something, from which Allah brings out a lot of good.

What about trading one wife for another? Yes, but don't ask for your money back.

> 4:20 If you wish to have one wife in the place of another and you have given either of them a heap of gold, do not take any of it back. Would you take it by recourse to injustice and manifest sin?

> 4:21 For how can you take it back, when you have been intimate one with the other, and they had taken from you a solemn pledge?

Daughters-in-Law

Daughters-in-law which your "adopted son" has divorce are eligible to an "adoptive father". The precedent was set by the Prophet himself. God's Messenger walked in on his daughter-in-law Zaynab when she was almost naked and he just had to have her. His adopted son divorced her so that the man he considered his father could marry her. A revelations concerning the "righteousness" of the whole thing followed by revelations confirming that the Prophet was in no way at fault.

> 33:37 And [remember] when you said to him whom Allah favoured and you favoured: (this is addressed to Zayd regarding his wife Zaynab) "Hold on to your wife and fear Allah", while you concealed within yourself what Allah would reveal and feared other men, whereas Allah had a better right to be feared by you. Then, when Zayd had satisfied his desire for her, We gave her to you in marriage; so that the believers should not be at fault, regarding the wives of their adopted sons, once they have satisfied their desire for them. For Allah's Command must be accomplished.

33:38 The Prophet was not at fault regarding what Allah prescribed for him as was His Way with those who were gone before. And Allah's Command is a pre-ordained decree.

33:39 Those who were delivering Allah's Message and feared Him, fearing none other than Allah. Allah suffices as a Reckoner.

Orphans and When a Son Is Not a Son

In Islam, if a problem, real or imagine, involves a female and it has nothing to do with her having sex outside marriage, than marriage is most often the solution. Marriage is also Allah's recommended course of action in dealing with female orphans. As you consider the following scattered noble sentiments concerning orphans, keep in mind that the male guardian of female orphans could, at his discretion, "marry such of the women as appeal to" him when they reached the age of nine (the age at which females can be married off under Islamic law i.e. the Sharia). By doing so, he maintains effective control of whatever property the female orphan might possess to use and dispose of at his discretion.

> 4:2 Render unto the orphans their property and do not exchange worthless things for good ones, and do not devour their property together with your property. That indeed is a great sin!

> 4:3 If you fear that you cannot deal justly with the orphans, then marry such of the women as appeal to you, two, three or four; but if you fear that you cannot be equitable, then only one, or what your right hands own (captives of war or slave-girls). That is more likely to enable you to avoid unfairness.

> 4:4 And give women their dowries as a free gift, but if they chose to give you anything of it, then consume it with enjoyment and pleasure.

> 4:5 But do not give the feeble-minded the property that Allah assigned to you as a means of livelihood. Provide for them therefrom, clothe them and speak kindly to them.

> 4:6 Test the orphans until they reach the age of marriage; then, if you discern in them sound judgement, deliver to

them their property; and do not consume it extravagantly and hastily before they come of age. He who is rich should be abstinent, and he, who is poor, should consume fairly. And when you deliver to them their property, call in witnesses thereon. God suffices as a Reckoner!

4:9 And let those who worry about the weak offspring they may leave behind them (after their death) be mindful [of the orphans]. Let them fear Allah and speak justly.

4:10 Those who devour the property of orphans unjustly, devour fire in their bellies, and they will burn in a blazing fire.

4:127 They consult you concerning women. Say: "Allah has instructed you concerning them, and concerning what is recited to you in the Book regarding orphan women for whom you do not give what is prescribed for them, although you wish to marry them, and concerning the weak children, and your duty to deal justly with the orphans (when considering the dowry and inheritance). For whatever good you do, Allah knows it very well."

Orphaned boys were almost unknown in the Arab world until Allah changed their status so that His Messenger could marry his adopted son's wife.

Marrying you son's former wife was taboo. It did not matter if he was adopted, the same ethical and moral restrictions applied as to a natural born son. Before Allah changed the status of adopted sons from sons to "brothers in religion", revelation 33:5, Arab fathers made no distinction between adopted sons and those they had fathered.

33:4 Allah did not create two hearts within the breast of any man; and He did not make your wives, whom you compare to your mothers' backs; and He did not make your [adopted] sons your sons in fact. That is your own claim, by your words of mouth. Allah speaks the truth and He guides to the Right Path.

33:5 Assign them to their own fathers. That is more equitable in the sight of Allah; but if you do not know their real fathers, then they are your brothers in religion, your adopted fellow Muslims. You are not at fault if you err therein; but only in what your hearts intend. Allah is ever All-Forgiving, All-Merciful.

Demoting adopted sons to "brothers in religion" made their wives, upon divorce, eligible to be taken in marriage by your "adoptive" father.

The revelation changing the relationship between adopted sons and their surrogate parent so that that God's Messenger could add to his collection of wives, concubines and slave-girls his former daughter-in-law have been interpreted to mean that Islam is against Western style adoption, resulting in an untold number of children in the Islamic world who have no one to call father.

Divorce and Who Gets the Kids

Divorce in the Koran is based on pre-Islamic laws and traditions, which must have been abysmal for Allah's revelations pertaining to the separation of legally married couples considered an improvement where women are concerned. Some of the revelations pertaining to divorce were said to have been introduced because of a woman pleading with the Prophet.

THE PLEADING WOMAN

58 Al-Mujadilah

In the Name of Allah,
the Compassionate, the Merciful

58:1 Allah has heard the words of that woman who disputes with you, concerning her husband, and complains to Allah, while Allah hears you both conversing. Allah is truly All-Hearing, All-Seeing.

The improvements introduced by Allah have mainly to do with the disposition of the dowry, which in Islam is the gift a husband makes to his new wife.

2:236 You incur no offence if you divorce women before the consummation of marriage or fixing the dowry. And provide for them in a rightful way: the wealthy according to his means, and the less fortunate according to his means. This is incumbent on the righteous.

> 2:237 If, however, you divorce them before the
> consummation of marriage, but after fixing the dowry, then
> [give them] half of the fixed dowry, unless they forgo that,
> or the man in whose hand is the marriage tie (the husband)
> forgoes his half. To forgo it is more righteous. And do not
> forget to be bountiful to each other. Allah sees what you do.

A husband does not need a reason to divorce any of his wives or
obtain anyone's permission to do so. He simply has to tell her "I
divorce you" and wait until his soon-to-be-divorced wife has
experienced three menstrual cycles and it's over. For a woman it is a
little more complicated. She can, however, simplify the whole process
and remain in Allah's good books if she agrees to pay her husband a
ransom. The price of freedom usually includes returning much of
what he has ever given her, including the dowry.

> 2:229 Divorce may be pronounced twice. Then they
> (women) are to be retained in a rightful manner or released
> with kindness. And it is unlawful for you [men] to take
> back anything of what you have given them unless both
> parties fear that they cannot comply with Allah's Bounds
> (by obeying His commands). If you fear that they cannot do
> that, then it is no offence if the woman ransoms herself
> [pays money to be set free]. Those are the bounds set by
> Allah. Do not transgress them. Those who transgress the
> bounds set by Allah are the wrongdoers.

"Divorce may be pronounced twice" in the preceding verse means
that the husband can divorce his wife three times. If he divorces her a
third time he can never take her back. A divorced woman is expected
to leave the family home after experiencing her third menstrual cycle
after being informed by her husband that they are no longer husband
and wife. Her former husband can allow her to stay longer if he
wishes, as long as it is not for ulterior motives, for example to obtain a
larger ransom.

> 2:231 If you divorce [your] women and they reach the end
> of their [waiting] period, retain them in an honourable
> manner or release them in an honourable manner. Do not,
> however, retain them for the sake of causing them harm
> and in order to commit aggression (by forcing them to
> ransom themselves, or by retaining them for a longer
> period). Whoever does that shall do wrong to himself. Do

not make a mockery of Allah's Revelations; and remember the Grace Allah has bestowed upon you, and the Book (the Koran) and the wisdom He has revealed to you in order to admonish you. Fear Allah and know that He knows everything.

Allah recommends that your divorced women be provided with an affordable provision. For how long, He does not say. For widows it is one year (2:240). They may have to pay for their sustenance depending on your interpretation of "affordable provision".

2:241 Divorce women should be provided with an affordable provision. This is incumbent on the righteous.

2:242 Thus Allah makes clear to you His Revelations, so that you may understand.

If you have never touched a lawfully-wedded spouse you can send her away on a moment's notice, as long as it is done in an *honourable* way.

33:49 O believers, if you marry believing women then divorce them, before touching them, you owe them no fixed term to reckon. So make provision for them and set them free in an honourable way.

I am assuming the following is not for the Prophet only.

THE DIVORCE

65 At-Talâq

In the Name of Allah,
the Compassionate, the Merciful

65:1 O Prophet, if you divorce your women, divorce them when they have completed their menstrual period. Calculate the period and fear Allah your Lord. Do not drive them out of their homes, and let them not go out, unless they have committed a manifest foul act. Those are the bounds of Allah. He who transgresses the bounds of Allah has surely wronged himself. You do not know, Allah may perhaps bring about something new after that.

If the divorce leaves the divorcer inconvenience in any way and he has followed Allah instructions to the letter, Allah will make it better.

As to the divorcee, she is on her own, unless her former husband decides to keep her in some other capacity.

> 65:2 Then, when they have reached their term, retain them honourably or part with them honourably, calling two just witnesses from among yourselves. Administer the witnessing to Allah Himself. By that is exhorted whoever believes in Allah and the Last Day. He who fears Allah, He will grant him a way out;

> 65:3 And He will provide for him from sources he could never conceive. He who puts his trust in Allah, Allah will be sufficient unto him. Allah shall attain His goal. Allah has meted out a measure for everything.

How long should you retain a woman or a girl who is not menstruating, such as a child-bride, or who is pregnant.

> 65:4 As for those of your women who have despaired of menstruation, if you are in doubt, then their term shall be three months; and those too who have not menstruated yet. As to those women with child, their term shall be upon delivering their burden. He who fears Allah, Allah will grant him relief in his affair.

> 65:5 That is Allah's Command, which He has sent down to you; and he who fears Allah, He will acquit him of his sins and amplify his reward.

Revelations about marriage made women out to be very much like chattel to be bargained for and disposed of at the buyer's discretion, except in the case of a soon-to-be-divorced spouse who is pregnant with her soon to be ex-husband's child. In this instance, her status goes from chattel to employee for the duration of the suckling, if she is willing to accept the wages offered by her former husband for the delivering to her newborn the sustenance he or she needs to survive. If not, then the former husband can chose another woman to suckle what is, in Allah's Sight, his child. In the Koran, a baby is created, perhaps exclusively from the man's sperm, with women being simply a receptacle, a warm place with plenty of water for the sperm to grow into a baby.

I do not know of any mother who would let another woman suckle her child because of a disagreement over wages; even after a divorce, which will undoubtedly leave her lacking many of life's bare necessities and dependent on the charity of others, mostly her family, unless she can quickly find another husband.

For all practical purposes, revelation 65:6 leaves a mother who cares about the child to whom she has just given birth with no negotiating position whatsoever, and it is not like a god of Allah's stature to pretend otherwise, unless I am missing something.

> 65:6 Put them up where you are lodged, according to your means, and do not badger them so as to make life difficult for them. If they are with child, support them until they deliver their burden; and if they suckle for you, then pay them their wages. Confer with each other honourably; but if you are at odds, let another woman suckle him.

From each according to his means but not to each according to her needs:

> 65:7 Let the man of means spent out of his means, and he whose provision has been constricted, spend out of what Allah gave him. Allah does not charge any soul except with what He gave it. Allah will cause relief to follow every hardship.

Allah is unclear, apart from that ransom thing, as to how a believing woman can get a divorce if she doesn't have the money to buy her freedom. Maybe that is why in countries that are governed by the Koran it is a matter decided by religious courts operating under the Sharia or Islamic Law, the law derived from the Koran and the sayings and example of the Prophet Muhammad. A woman seeking a divorce will usually appeal to an all-male Sharia Tribunal stating her reason for wanting a divorce. It must be a compelling reason for a divorce to be granted for Allah prefers reconciliation.

> 4:35 And If you fear a breach between the two (the husband and wife), then send forth for an arbiter from his relatives and another arbiter from her relatives. If they both desire reconciliation, Allah will bring them together. Allah is indeed all knowing, Well-Informed.

Allah favours reconciliation even if a spouse has been mistreated or fears being mistreated by her husband. What Allah favours you ignore at your risk and peril. Revelation 4:128 is an effective way of eliminating battering or other forms of abuse as grounds for granting a wife's request for a divorce. Revelation 4:128 is also the logical consequence of revelation 4:34 which grants a husband the unassailable right to beat his wives "... Hence righteous women are obedient, guarding the unseen which Allah has guarded. And those of them that you fear might rebel, admonish them and abandon them in their beds and beat them."

> 4:128 And if a woman fears maltreatment or aversion from her husband, they would not commit an offence if they are reconciled amicably; reconciliation is best. Souls are prone to avarice, and if you are charitable and if you ward off evil, He is surely Well-Aware of what you do!

To get her divorce a wife must usually agree to give up all or part of the dowry, the amount dependent on her reason for seeking a divorce, as compensation to her husband for leaving him. Allah promises that if they do separate, He will ensure that both former husband and wife will be provided for.

> 4:130 And if they separate, Allah will give each one plenty of His Abundance; and Allah is Munificent and Wise.

> 4:131 And to Allah belongs what is in the heavens and on earth. We have enjoined those who received the Book before you, as well as yourselves: "Fear Allah, and if you disbelieve, surely to Allah belongs what is the heavens and on earth. Allah is All-Sufficient, Praiseworthy."

A husband's wealth remains largely undiminished because of a divorce; and in fact, may increase, not only because of the return of all or part of the dowry but the ransom that he may demand and obtain for giving a wife her freedom. As to what a recently divorced woman can expect from Allah's Abundance, it is far from clear.

Under Islamic Law, the divorced mother usually gets custody of any sons under seven years of age and daughters who have not reached puberty. When sons reach the age of seven and daughters reach puberty (have become valuable commodities) custody usually reverts to the father.

Can a divorced couple get re-married? Yes, if the former wife, in the interim, has married, consummated the marriage and then been divorced by her latest husband. If the former husband was impotent, the Prophet ruled, that she could not remarry; in effect, condemning her to never knowing the intimacy of intercourse again.

Narrated Aisha: The wife of Rifa'a Al-Qurazi came to the

Prophet and said, "I was Rifa'a's wife, but he divorced me and it was a final irrevocable divorce. Then I married Abdur Rahman bin Az-Zubair but he is impotent." The Prophet asked her "Do you want to remarry Rifa'a? You cannot unless you had a complete sexual relation with your present husband." *Bukhari*

Yahya related to me from Malik… that Rifa'a ibn Simwal divorced his wife, Tamima bint Wahb, in the time of the messenger of Allah three times. She then married 'Abd ar-Rahman ibn az-Zubayr and he turned from her and could not consummate the marriage and so he parted from her. Rifa'a wanted to marry her again and it was mentioned to the Messenger of Allah, and he forbade him to marry her. He said, 'She is not halal for you until she has tasted the sweetness of intercourse.' *Al-Muwatta 28 7.17b*

The most current former husband should not interfere with a former wife's plans to marry a former spouse.

2:230 If he divorces her, she shall not be lawful to him again until she has married another husband. If the latter divorces her, then it is no offence if they go back to each other, if they both think that they shall keep within Allah's Bounds. Those are Allah's Bounds which He makes clear to men who have knowledge.

2:232 If you divorce your women and they reach the end of their [waiting] period, do not prevent them from marrying their [former] husbands if they agree among themselves in a rightful manner. With this are admonished those who believe in Allah and the Last Day; it is better and more decent for you. Allah knows and you do not.

~~~~~~~~~~~~~~~~

There is another type of divorce mentioned in some translations; example Yusuf Ali's translation of verse 58:3.

58:3 But those who divorce their wives by Zihar, then wish to go back on the words they uttered,- (It is ordained that such a one) should free a slave before they touch each other: Thus are ye admonished to perform: and Allah is well-acquainted with (all) that ye do.

A divorce by Zihar is the equivalent of saying ""You are like our mother's back." A person who has said his wife was like his mother's back who could not afford to free a slave, or did not have one to set free, could perform one of the two prescribed penances, after which it was legal for him to touch the woman he had Zihared (sic).

> 58:4 As for him who does not have the means, he should fast two consecutive months, before they can touch each other; and he who cannot not should feed sixty poor persons. That is prescribed that you may believe in Allah and His Messenger and these are the bounds of Allah. The unbelievers shall have a very painful punishment.

Spinsters and Prostitutes

Allah, in the following revelations, makes his views on spinsterhood, pre-marital sex, the emancipation of slaves and abstinence crystal clear. He is less forthcoming as to whether a man forcing a slave-girl into prostitution or who profits from his slaves prostituting themselves will face any sanctions.

> 24:32 Encourage the unmarried among you and the righteous among your servants and maids to marry. If they are poor, Allah will enrich them from His Bounty. Allah is All-Embracing, All-Knowing.

> 24:33 Let those who do not find the means to marry be abstinent, till Allah enriches them from his Bounty. Those whom your right hands own and who wish to pay for their emancipation, conclude a contract with them, if you know that there is some good in them, and give them of Allah's wealth which He gave you. Do not force your slave-girls into prostitution, if they wish to be chaste, in order to seek the fleeting goods of this life. Whoever forces them, surely Allah, after their being forced, is Forgiving, Merciful.

> 24:34 And We have sent down to you signs making everything clear, and an example of those who have gone before you, and an exhortation to the God-fearing.

While prostitution per se is forbidden, the Prophet did allow for temporary marriages so that men at war with no female captives to rape could still have sex. Except under extraordinary circumstances Sunnis consider temporary marriages haram while Shiites have made it part of their legal code and accessible to just about everyone. A few hadiths on the subject of temporary marriages:

> Narrated Abdullah: We used to participate in the holy wars carried on by the Prophet and we had no women (wives) with us. So we said (to the Prophet). "Shall we castrate ourselves?" But the Prophet forbade us to do that and thenceforth he allowed us to marry a woman (temporarily) by giving her even a garment, and then he recited: "O you who believe! Do not make unlawful the good things which Allah has made lawful for you." Qur'an 5:87 *Bukhari*

> Sabra Juhanni reported: Allah's Messenger (may peace be upon him) permitted temporary marriage for us. So I and another person went out and saw a woman of Bana 'Amir, who was like a young long-necked she-camel. We presented ourselves to her (for contracting temporary marriage), whereupon she said: What dower would you give me? I said: My cloak. And my companion also said: My cloak. And the cloak of-my companion was superior to my cloak, but I was younger than he. So when she looked at the cloak of my companion she liked it, and when she cast a glance at me I looked more attractive to her. She then said: Well, you and your cloak are sufficient for me. I remained with her for three nights, and then Allah's Messenger (may peace be upon him) said: He who has any such woman with whom he had contracted temporary marriage, he should let her off. *Sahih Muslim*

The Suckling Imperative

According to Ya'qubi, an Arab historian and geographer, Muhammad once said that his first wet nurse was the nastiest of women and that she would burn for all eternity in the fires of Hell. To quench her thirst she would only have the small amount of milk she allowed him to suckle in the days following his birth. The Prophet also reported having a vision of Hell where women who had not suckled their children had snakes biting at their breast.

The revelations on how long a mother or a wet-nurse must suckle a child and what the parents must do if they choose to shorten the weaning period decreed by Allah may have had something to do with God's Messenger's awareness that he had not been adequately breastfed when he was a baby, and Allah wishing that such a calamity be visited on as few children as possible.

> 2:233 Mothers shall suckle their children for two whole years; [that is] for those who wish to complete the suckling. Those to whom the children are born (the fathers) shall maintain and clothe them kindly. No soul is charged beyond its capacity. No mother should suffer on account of her child and he to whom a child is born should not suffer on account of his child. The same [duties (the maintenance and clothing of divorced women)] devolve upon the [father's] heir (if the heir is a child and has a guardian the latter would be charged with those duties). But they commit no offence if by mutual agreement and following consultation they choose to wean the child. You also commit no offence if you engage wet-nurses, provided that you give them what you promised to give kindly. Fear Allah and know that Allah has knowledge of what you do.

If the decreed suckling period is 24 months then Allah, in the following verse where He reveals that the gestation and weaning period total 30 months, has underestimated the gestation period of the human fetus by three months (30 - 24 = 6 months gestation time).

> 46:15 We have commanded man to be kind to his parents; his mother bore him painfully and delivered him painfully, his gestation and weaning totalling thirty months. When he is fully grown and turns forty, he will say: "Lord, inspire me to be thankful for the favour, with which You have favoured me and favoured my parents; and to do a righteous deed, well-pleasing to You. Grant me righteousness in my progeny; I have truly repented to You and one of those who submit."

The Prophet ruled that a woman who suckled an adult male who was not a close relation made marriage not only impossible for him but undesirable; he became the equivalent of a close relation and therefore could spend time with her alone.

> The Ulema'A'isha (Allah be pleased with her) reported that Salim, the freed slave of Abu Hadhaifa, lived with him and his family in their house. She (i. e. the daughter of Suhail came to Allah's Apostle (may peace be upon him) and said:

Salim has attained (puberty) as men attain, and he understands what they understand, and he enters our house freely, I, however, perceive that something (rankles) in the heart of Abu Hudhaifa, whereupon Allah's Apostle (may peace be upon him) said to her: Suckle him and you would become unlawful for him, and (the rankling) which Abu Hudhaifa feels in his heart will disappear. She returned and said: So I suckled him, and what (was there) in the heart of Abu Hudhaifa disappeared. *Sahih Muslim*

Polygamy

Polygamy! Is The Koran For or Against? In the following verse, already quoted, Allah appears to grant men the right to marry up to four wives if he can treat them all equally:

4:3 If you fear that you cannot deal justly with the orphans, then marry such of the women as appeal to you, two, three or four; but if you fear that you cannot be equitable, then only one, or what your right hands own (captives of war or slave-girls). This is more likely to enable you to avoid unfairness.

In a later verse Allah states that it is impossible for a man who has more than one wife to treat them equally.

4:129 You will never be able to treat wives equally, even if you are bent on doing that. So do not turn away altogether [from any of them] leaving her, like one in suspense; and if you do justice [to her] and guard against evil. He (Allah) is surely All-Forgiving, Merciful.

Muhammad 'Abduh, (1849:1905) "Egyptian jurist, religious scholar and liberal reformer, regarded as the founder of Islamic Modernism" (Wiki) argued that these two verses taken together means that the Koran is against polygamy. The Prophet would not allow his son-in-law Ali to take another wife after Fatima. This also suggest that polygamy is not a hard and fast rule.

Narrated Al-Miswar bin Makhrama: I heard Allah's Apostle who was on the pulpit, saying, "Banu Hisham bin Al-Mughira have requested me to allow them to marry their daughter to Ali bin Abu Talib, but I don't give permission, and will not give permission unless 'Ali bin Abi Talib divorces my daughter in order to marry their daughter, because Fatima is a part of my body, and I hate what she hates to see, and what hurts her, hurts me." *Bukhari*

The Perfect Wife

Previously, we talked about how Allah made believing women and girls dependent on men for everything from the bare necessities of life to simple luxuries, thereby making them beholden to men, especially older, wealthy men and men in positions of power. We also presented a revelation, verse 2:223 where Allah informs believing men that "Your women are tillage for you. So get to your tillage whenever you like."

The Koran does contain a number of verses which impose some mostly minor restrictions on the beneficiaries of this "carte-blanche" dispensation when it comes to the sexual demands they can make of the fair and vulnerable sex. Verse 2:222, for example, forbids a man from demanding sex from his wife if she is menstruating.

> 2:222 And they ask you about menstruation say: "It is an impurity." So keep away from women during their menstruation and do not approach them (do not have sexual relations with them) until they are clean. Once they get clean get to them as Allah commanded you. Allah loves the repentant and loves those who purify themselves.

This is not out of consideration for his spouse but because in Allah's eyes she is unclean, not only for sex but for prayer.

There are a few other occasions that have nothing to do with a woman's reproductive cycle, where Allah prohibits a man, for a precise period of time, from demanding sex from his lawfully wedded spouse. For instance, a husband must wait at least four months before being intimate with his wife if he previously swore that he would never have sex with her again but changes his mind.

> 2:226 Those who swear not to approach their wives should wait for four months; then if they change their minds, Allah is Forgiving, Merciful.

2:227 If they resolve on divorce, Allah is All-Hearing, All-Knowing.

The time penalties for believing men and Allah's prohibition against a man having sex with a menstruating spouse notwithstanding, a believing wife cannot refuse her husband's request for sex. As explained in *It Is God's Will,* if she does, she not only risks a beating at the hands of her husband but also eternal damnation. Revisiting the relevant portion of verse 4:34 quoted in its entirety in *Who Gets What.*

> 4:34 … Hence righteous women are obedient, guarding the unseen which Allah has guarded. <u>And those of them that you fear might rebel, admonish them and abandon them in their beds and beat them</u>. Should they obey you, do not seek a way of harming them; for Allah is Sublime and Great!

Why would God, not only allow, but seemingly encourage a husband to beat his wife for a variety of reasons including, in my opinion, refusing him access to her body? Could it be unintended consequences of God's Messenger discovering the joys of a varied sex life, especially sex with younger women and girls when he was past his prime? Of course, the Prophet Muhammad's accumulation of wives, concubines and slave-girls when he was well into his middle-age years could also have been attributable to the Prophet's altruistic nature.

God's Messenger when it came to the believers was, for the most part, a caring, thoughtful man. The kind of man that would have been pre-disposed to care for those he perceived as the most vulnerable members of society: widows, young women and teenaged girls. The best way to do this, in the Prophet's time, was to marry them or make them members of your household, and this was, after all, during a time of war when Muslims were fighting for their very survival.

A Man and His Wives

The Prophet Muhammad had fourteen official wives. For twenty-three years God's Messenger was married to one woman, Khadijah. It was Khadijah's third marriage, the Prophet's first. He was twenty-five, she was forty when they tied the knot. We are told he was faithful to her and loved her very much. I believe that. He would even have Adam, of Adam and Eve fame, pay her the supreme compliment. From *La vie de Mahomet* by Virgil Gheorghiu, page 79, my translation.

> "One of the things that Allah gave to Muhammad and not to me, was a wife like Khadijah who helped him carry out God's will, while my own wife, Eve only encouraged me to disobey (God)." *Adam*

Khadijah gave birth to two, maybe three sons depending on who you read, and four girls. All of the Prophet's sons would die in infancy. The youngest daughter, Fatima, was the only offspring of the Prophet Muhammad to have descendants. She was married to Ali, the fourth caliph (the fourth successor to the Prophet).

Shi'ites (Shi'ites means partisan or faction of Ali) maintain that the proper successor of the Prophet Muhammad was Ali followed by the son of Ali and Fatima; Hussain. Shia's consider the first three caliphs who succeeded the Prophet Muhammad, and those who followed Ali, usurpers.

The Sunni-Shi'ite division of Islam originated because of this succession dispute shortly after the death of the Prophet Muhammad in 632 A.D. and the murder of Ali and his son Hussain. Every day Sunnis and Shi'ites faithful are reminded of their irreconcilable divergence in the simple declaration of faith that is part of their daily prayers, the Shahadah.

The Sunni version:

> I declare there is no god except God, and I declare that Muhammad is the Messenger of God

The Shi'ite version:

> There is no god but Allah, Muhammad is the Messenger of Allah, Ali is the Friend of Allah. The Successor of the Messenger of Allah and his first Caliph.

After the death of his first wife Khadijah, the Prophet did not marry again until he was past fifty. His next wife was again a widow. He then married Aisha the daughter of his good friend and close collaborator Abu Bakr. Aisha was the first child born to parents who were believers. The progeny of believers are born Muslim. The founder of Islam would marry the first child born a Muslim.

Traditional Muslim scholars and clerics maintain that a grateful Abu Bakr offered his nine-year-old daughter, with whom the Prophet

Muhammad had fallen in love, to the Prophet to cement his relationship with God's Messenger. Ayaan Hirsi Ali, in *The Caged Virgin*, writes that Aisha's father pleaded with the Prophet to wait until his daughter reached adulthood before marrying her.

> ... he fell in love with Aisha, his best friend's nine-year-old daughter. Her father said: "Please wait until she has reached adulthood." But Muhammad would not wait... In other words, Muhammad teaches us that it is fine to take away your best friend's child. By our Western standards Muhammad is a perverse man. *Ayaan Hirsi Ali. The Caged Virgin, p. 81*

A hadith recorded by Bukhari would appear to support Ali's assertion that Aisha's father was not keen on marrying his daughter to a man of his generation:

> Narrated 'Ursa: The Prophet asked Abu Bakr for 'Aisha's hand in marriage. Abu Bakr said "But I am your brother." The Prophet said, "You are my brother in Allah's religion and His Book, but she (Aisha) is lawful for me to marry."

Aisha's recollection of her wedding day would suggest that the bride was not yet a teenager when she joined God's Messenger on the matrimonial mat. The fact that Aisha's wedding was not celebrated, the meaning of "Neither a camel nor a sheep was slaughtered on behalf of me" in the following account by Tabari, may be an indication that God's Messenger was not proud of what he was about to do and did not want it to be an example for others. Or, that his people did not approve of their 50+ tribesman marrying and having sex with a child.

> My mother came to me while I was being swung on a swing between two branches and got me down. My nurse took over and wiped my face with some water and started leading me. When I was at the door she stopped so I could catch my breath. I was brought in while Muhammad was sitting on a bed in our house. My mother made me sit on his lap. The other men and women got up and left. The Prophet consummated his marriage with me in my house when I was nine years old. Neither a camel nor a sheep was slaughtered on behalf of me. *Tabari IX:131*

The late Ayatollah Khomeini and Islamic law would also appear to support Hirsi Ali's claim of Aisha's age when she lost her virginity to God's Messenger. Sharia Law is based on the Koran and the Prophet's *Sunnah* (the sayings or hadiths and example of the Prophet Muhammad including the silent approval of actions done in his presence). For the believer, the Koran is the literal word of God and the divine instructions it contains cannot be questioned and must be rigorously adhered to. The same can be said for the Prophet's Sunnah as long as it does not contradict the Koran.

God's Messenger, for the believers, is the personification of the perfect human being. Being perfect, like his patron, he *cannot be faulted for anything he has said or done*. When the Ayatollah Khomeini lowered the age at which a girl could be legally married to nine years of age[10], he may simply have been making Iranian law conform to the Prophet's example. In Islam, there is no higher law than the Koran and the Prophet's Sunnah and for following the law laid down by Allah and His Messenger no Muslim *can be faulted*.

While the claim that God's Messenger had sexual intercourse with a nine year old girl can never be conclusively proven, it is reasonable to assume that Aisha moved into the Prophet's house when the engagement was announced or after her wedding based on a previously quoted observation by Khomeini that "it was better in the eyes of God if a girl started menstruating in the home of her husband instead of that of her father ... "

If I dwell at some length on the marriage of the young Aisha to a middle-age man, it is because this child, this girl was probably the most significant influence on God and His Messenger's view of women; a view to which we will return later. Also, as already mentioned, for Muslims, the Prophet Muhammad is the embodiment of the perfect human being, his conduct beyond reproach. A reputation so highly valued that, as demonstrated during the "cartoon protest", you question the basis of that reputation at your risk and peril. Muslims, especially men, are expected to closely follow the Prophet's example in how they conduct themselves in private and in public. It is the opinion of Ayaan Hirsi Ali that, if her interpretation

---

[10] In May 2006, the Iranian Parliament voted to make it compulsory for girls under the age of 15 and boys under 18 to have court approval to get married. This vote was quashed by the Guardian Council which is responsible for ensuring that any laws passed by Parliament are compatible with Islam. The clerics on the Council ruled that such a move would break Islamic law which sets the minimum marriage age at 9 for girls and 14 for boys.

of the historical record is the correct one, by western standards, the believers are following the example of a "perverse man."

After Aisha, God's Messenger would marry many, many times over. The official number is fourteen wives not counting slave-girls[11] and concubines. Some marriages were entered into to cement alliances; others may have been the Prophet's way of taking care of the widows and orphans of men who had died defending or spreading Islam. The beautiful twenty year old widow Hafsah would become wife number four. God's Messenger was fifty-four. All of the Prophet's young wives were reputed to be women of exceptional beauty. Over the next ten years he would marry again ten times. His last wife was, depending again on who you believe, between thirty and thirty-nine years his junior; his second to last wife was forty-seven years younger. This may not be that surprising. After Aisha, God's Messenger, in a hadith recorded by Bukhari, did expressed a preference for younger women, girls actually:

> Narrated Jabir bin Abdullah: While we were returning from a Ghazwa (Holy Battle) with the Prophet, I started driving my camel fast, as it was a lazy camel A rider came behind me and pricked my camel with a spear he had with him, and then my camel started running as fast as the best camel you may see. Behold! The rider was the Prophet himself. He said, 'What makes you in such a hurry?" I replied, I am newly married " He said, "Did you marry a virgin or a matron? I replied, "A matron." He said, "Why didn't you marry a young girl so that you may play with her and she with you?" When we were about to enter (Medina), the Prophet said, "Wait so that you may enter (Medina) at night so that the lady of unkempt hair may comb her hair and the

---

[11] A hadith on how believers decided if the Prophet had taken a wife or a slave:

Narrated Anas: The Prophet stayed for three days between Khaibar and Medina, and there he consummated his marriage to Safiyya bint Huyai. I invited the Muslims to the wedding banquet in which neither meat nor bread was offered. He ordered for leather dining-sheets to be spread, and dates, dried yoghurt and butter were laid on it, and that was the Prophet's wedding banquet. The Muslims wondered, "Is she (Saffiyya) considered as his wife or his slave girl?" Then they said, "If he orders her to veil herself, she will be one of the mothers of the Believers; but if he does not order her to veil herself, she will be a slave girl. So when the Prophet proceeded from there, he spared her a space behind him (on his she-camel) and put a screening veil between her and the people. *Bukhari*

one whose husband has been absent may shave her pubic region.

The Prophet also took a number of concubines from among his slave-girls, including the beautiful Rayhanah, the aforementioned widow of the Beni Qurayzah Jewish clan of Medina whose men and teenaged boys were beheaded for strategic reasons.

A middle-age man, even in the best of emotional and physical condition, would have difficulties controlling this ménage of post and pre-pubescent girls and young women in the prime of their sexual life. As the Messenger of God, he could not depend on soldiers or others to keep his collection of females from wandering or being tempted by young men of their generation. He had to solve his female management difficulties some other way. The solution was obvious. He was God's Messenger after all and he not only listened to God, God, listened to him. In revelation 4:3 Allah put a limit of four wives per husband.

The Prophet wanted to exceed this God ordained matrimonial limit. Not a problem. Allah provided a revelation making the whole thing legal ... *for His Messenger*. Here is the verse which granted God's Messenger an unlimited number of wives and concubines.

> 33:50 O Prophet, we have made lawful, for you, your wives, whose dowry you have paid, what your right hand owns (slave-girls) out of the spoils of war that Allah gave you, the daughters of your paternal uncles, the daughters of your paternal aunts, the daughters of your maternal uncles, the daughters of your maternal aunts who emigrated with you, and any believing woman who gives herself freely to the Prophet, if the Prophet desires to marry her, <u>granted exclusively to you, but not the believers</u>. We know what We have prescribed for them regarding their wives and what their right hands own, so that you may not be at fault. Allah is All-Forgiving, Merciful.

Islamic scholar Yahiya Emerick does not see the preceding verse as giving the Prophet the right to exceed the matrimonial limit. He writes that the revelation, setting the limit at four wives, came after God's Messenger had married the last of his fourteen wives. Since none of Allah's revelations are dated, it is anybody's guess which came first.

For the women who gave themselves "freely" (which I interpret

as allowing the Prophet to break one of Allah's most strict prohibition
i.e. sex outside marriage) having shared the Prophet's bed should be
reward enough if His Messenger decided to send them on their way
with little or no compensation.

> 33:51 You may defer any of them you wish, and take in any
> of them that you wish or any that you may have cut off. So
> you are not liable to reproach, For thus it is more likely that
> they will be delighted and will not grieve, but be content
> with what you have given each one of them. Allah knows
> what is within your hearts; and Allah is All-Knowing,
> Clement[12].

Allah, it is clear, was extremely concerned that His Messenger be
sexually fulfilled[13], so it should come as no surprise when in a
revelation he raised the matrimonial limit for His Messenger *and His
Messenger only.* For the Prophet who, as we mentioned earlier, was
already pre-disposed to care for widows, young women and girls,
which he perceived as the most vulnerable members of society, this
was perhaps too much of an indulgence. This act of kindness for His
Messenger, in my opinion, would lead to the wife management
problem which would compel Allah, on numerous occasions, to
intervene to help His Messenger with his wives. The only problem;
God's solutions for His Messenger became every Muslim man's
solution when it came to "managing" their household.

It is perhaps unfortunate that the Prophet Muhammad did not
heed Allah's warning that you should only take as many wives as

---

[12] Perhaps not surprisingly, of the few people for whom the Prophet could ask
forgiveness, were the women who paid him homage.

> 60:12 O Prophet, if believing women come to you to pay you homage,
> pledging not to associate anything with Allah, steal, commit adultery, kill
> their children, come up with a lie they invent between their hands and feet
> (allege that an illegitimate child is their husband's) or disobey you in any
> honourable matter, then accept their homage and ask Allah's Forgiveness for
> them. Allah indeed is All-Forgiving, All-Merciful.

[13] In a Bukhari hadith Aisha offers a rather wry comment about Allah hastily
fulfilling her husband's wishes when it came to sex after this revelation was received.

> Narrated Aisha: I used to look down upon those ladies who had given
> themselves to Allah's Apostle and I used to say, "Can a lady give herself (to a
> man)?" But when Allah revealed: "You (O Muhammad) can postpone (the
> turn of) whom you will of them (your wives), and you may receive any of
> them whom you will; and there is no blame on you if you invite one whose
> turn you have set aside (temporarily).' (33.51) I said (to the Prophet), "I feel
> that your Lord hastens in fulfilling your wishes and desires." *Bukhari 60.675*

you can handle, or that Allah did not force His Messenger to stay within the prescribed limit like everybody else. After all, God's Messenger, like every believing man, could still have as many slave-girls and concubines as he could handle. If Allah had tempered His Messenger's altruistic endeavours when it came to helping the weaker sex, Muslim women would probably be much better off today.

When it came to sex there would be one law for the believers and another law for God's Messenger. Is it Allah or is it His Messenger who realises that He may have gone too far? Is the following verse meant to reassure the believers that no further exceptions will be granted the Prophet when it comes to the females that he can bring into his household or with whom he can have intimate relations?

> 33:52 Thereafter, other women are not lawful to you, nor is substituting other wives for them, even if you admire their beauty, except for what your right hand owns. Allah is Watchful over everything.

Why would God in a book meant to be a moral guide for mankind for centuries to come, spend so much time on the sex life of just one man? If that sex life was to be held up as an example to the faithful then perhaps it would have its place in such as book, but as an exception to Allah's rules for the ordinary believer?

In the Prophet's House

In verse 24:27 Allah warned the believers not to "enter houses other than your own before you ask leave and greet their occupants." He placed additional restrictions as to when you can enter the Prophet's houses, how to behave once inside and what type of interaction is permitted, if any, with the Prophet's wives while inside His Messenger's house.

> 33:53 O believers, do not enter the houses of the Prophet, unless you are invited to a meal, without awaiting the hour; but if you are invited, then enter; but when you have eaten, disperse, without lingering for idle talk. That is vexing to the Prophet who might be wary of you, but Allah is not wary of the truth. If you ask them (the wives of the Prophet) for an object, ask them from behind a curtain. That is purer for your hearts and theirs. You should never hurt the

Messenger of Allah, <u>nor take his wives in marriage after him</u>. That is truly abominable in the sight of Allah.

33:54 Whether you reveal a thing or conceal, Allah has knowledge of everything.

Allah ends this curious revelation, verse 33:53, with an admonishment for the men, warning them to keep their distance from His Messenger's wives after His Messenger has left this world on route to a better one. Why would Allah, in a book meant to guide humanity till the end of time, include a prohibition which disappeared with the passing of the Prophet's last wife. It only served to make His Messenger out to be a jealous obsessive man, a man who would seek to control the lives of his widows from beyond the grave[14] .

For Muslim women, having sex with a man other than their husband is flirting with a gruesome death and risking spending an eternity on fire in the depth of Allah's Hell. The interdiction against taking "his wives in marriage after him" is equivalent to condemning the Prophet's young wives to never enjoying being intimate with a man again after his passing.

A Taste of Honey

Allah's revelations to His Messenger when it came to helping him control his wives, slave-girls and concubines give us a view into the mind of the Almighty when it comes to women. Here is what most would consider a trivial case of wife management in which the Almighty feels compelled to intervene.

The situation is this: the Prophet has told one of his wives, in secrecy, that he has eaten some honey. This wife then tells another of his wives that God's Messenger has eaten some honey. Allah, who sees and hears all, decides to tell His Messenger part of what he saw and heard. We are not told about the part Allah leaves out, even though this is the part that seems to hold the key to the story, unless the story is really about honey. It is again a somewhat infantile story which could easily have been dismissed if Allah had not chosen this opportunity to express his views on what constitutes the perfect wife.

---

[14] Making matters worse, the Prophet's widows were deprived of most of their inheritance by his immediate successor Abu Bakr who claimed God's Messenger had told him that after his death, if they were in need, they should "accept alms."

Here is how it all went down. First, Allah informs His Messenger of part of the conversation He has overheard.

> 66:3 And when the Prophet confided to one of his wives a certain matter (his eating of honey); and she divulged it, and Allah disclosed it to him too, He made known part of it, but withheld the other part. Then, when he told her about it, she said: "Who told you this?" He said: "The All-Knowing, All-Informed told me."

Allah suspects a conspiracy against His Messenger. To put an end to the gossip about the honey He informs the two women of the formidable force allied against them: God himself, most of the believers and all the angels, including the mighty Gabriel support the Prophet Muhammad. This has to be about more than one wife divulging to another that their husband-in-common has eaten some honey for Allah to put His own prestige on the line and to throw in everything but the kitchen sink to force the two women to keep quiet.

> 66:4 If you two (the two wives of the Prophet) repent onto Allah, then your hearts will have certainly inclined; but if you band together against him, then Allah is his Master. Gabriel, the righteous among the believers and the angels thereupon are his supporters, too.

Then the really big threat – especially in the Prophet Muhammad's time – *divorce*. Allah will grant His Messenger a divorce so that He may give him in exchange "the perfect wife" which He proceeds to describe.

> 66:5 Perhaps, his Lord will, if he divorces you, give him in exchange wives better than you, submissive, believing, obedient, penitent, devout, fasting, either previously married or virgins.

Do you measure up? Allah follows his instructions about how wives should behave with the usual threat about burning you to a crisp if His instructions are not scrupulously followed.

> 66:6 O believers, guard yourselves and your families against a Fire whose fuel is people and stones; its overseers are harsh, terrible angels who do not disobey what Allah commands, but will do what they are commanded.

A Child Bride's Indiscretion

After the tasting of the honey calamity came the incident with the Prophet's child bride. It seems the lovely Aisha had wandered into the desert and got lost only to be rescued by a young man who brought her back to Medina ... *the next day*. Needless to say, this started people talking. Talk, if revelations pertaining to this incident are to be believed, that really distressed the Messenger. Again, Allah intervened, not only to vouch for Aisha's faithfulness, but also to make sure that none of the Prophet's wives would ever put His Messenger in an embarrassing situation again – in a position where he would be the object of gossip, "chatter" as Allah calls it.

It is worth giving you all of the verses in this series so you will have a real appreciation of the mind-set of Allah and His Messenger in relation to the beautiful, young Aisha's alleged indiscretion under an Arabian moon more than a thousand years ago.

> 24:10 And, but for Allah's Bounty towards you and His Mercy and that Allah is a remitter of sins and is All-Wise;

> 24:11 Those who spread the slander (against Aisha, wife of the Prophet, according to the commentators) are a band of you. Do not reckon it an evil for you; rather it is a good thing for you. Everyone of them will be credited with the sin he has earned, and he who bore the brunt of it shall have a terrible punishment.

> 24:12 Would that the believers, men and women, when you heard it (the slander) had though well of themselves saying: "This is manifest slander!"

> 24:13 And would that they had brought forth four witnesses [to vouch for it]! But since they did not bring any witnesses, those are, in Allah's sight, the real liars.

> 24:14 And but for Allah's Bounty to you and His Mercy, in this world and the next, you would have been visited, due to your chatter, by a terrible punishment.

While Allah makes a big deal of the whole situation with Aisha, He readily admits that His Messenger's friends and neighbours thought the situation with Aisha was no big deal.

> 24:15 Since you received it on your tongues and you uttered with your mouths what you had no knowledge of, deeming

it a simple matter; whereas in Allah's Sight it was very grave.

But they would be wrong; this was not a trivial matter.

24:16 And would that, upon hearing it, you were to say: "It is not for us to speak about this. Glory be to You; this is truly a great calumny."

And let us never talk about this again.

24:17 Allah admonishes you never to return to the like of this, if you are real believers.

24:18 And Allah expounds clearly for you the Signs. Allah is all Knowing, Wise.

Aisha's alleged sexual indiscretion appears to be the source of Allah's condemnation of what he sees as the spread of indecency among the believers, what Muslim clerics today would call *western libertinism*. His usual condemnation is followed by His usual promise of a very painful punishment in the next world and, in a somewhat rare occurrence, also a promise of a very painful punishment in this one.

24:19 Indeed, those who love to see indecency spread among the believers will have in this world and the next a very painful punishment. Allah knows, but you do not know.

24:20 And but for Allah's Bounty to you and His Mercy and that Allah is truly Clement and Merciful;

24:21 O believers, do not follow in the footsteps of Satan; for he who follows in the footsteps of Satan, simply bids to indecency and disrepute. But for Allah's Bounty to you and His Mercy, no one of you would have ever been pure; but Allah purifies whomever He pleases. Allah is All-Hearing, All Knowing.

A reminder from Allah about forgiveness; it's a quid pro quo thing.

24:22 Let not the bounteous and wealthy among you swear off giving freely to kinsmen, the destitute and the Emigrants in the Path of Allah. Let them pardon and forgive. Do you not wish that Allah should forgive you? Allah is All-Forgiving, Merciful.

It was the tradition of the Arabs of the Peninsula, during the time of the Prophet, that if there was any doubt about a wife's faithfulness she was divorced on the spot then stoned to death. In Virgil Gheorghiu's biography of the Prophet, *La Vie de Mahomet*, Ali, the son-in-law of the Prophet suggest as much in his remark to God's Messenger that "Allah has not placed any limits on the choice of a wife. They are plentiful." (my translation of « Allah n'a point limité le choix de femmes. Elles sont nombreuses »)[15]

It is obvious that the Prophet cherished his child-bride and did not wish to part with her. This may explain Allah's attack on those who would "slander married women."

> 24:23 Surely those who slander married women, who are heedless and believing, are accursed in this world and the next, and they shall have a terrible punishment.

And who will be your accusers? On Judgement Day, your limbs, the organs by which you sinned will speak and tell everyone how you used them to sin against Allah, and in this particular instance, His Messenger.

> 24:24 On the Day when their tongues, their hands and their feet shall bear witness against them, regarding what they used to do.

> 24:25 On that Day Allah will pay them their just dues and they will know that Allah is the Manifest Truth.

A verse, somewhat off-topic, where Allah makes his views known on how some men and women should be paired based on whether they've been bad or good.

> 24:26 Foul women for foul men, and foul men for foul women; and good women for good men, and good men for good women. Those are acquitted of the burden of what they say; they will have forgiveness and a generous provision.

In this extraordinary and revealing series of verses Allah also has a few instructions for men perchance they might accidentally come into

---

[15] Aisha would not forgive Ali. Gheorghiu maintains that this remark was central to the great schism in Islam that saw the rise of Shi'a as a competing sect to the Sunnis.

contact with an unsupervised woman to whom they are not related or married.

> 24:27 O believers, do not enter houses other than your own before you ask leave and greet their occupants. This is better for you, that perchance you may remember well.

> 24:28 If you find no one in them, do not enter until you are given permission; and if it is said to you: "Go back", then go back. That is purer for you, and Allah knows well what you do.

> 24:29 It is no offence for you to enter uninhabited houses in which you have some means of enjoyment. Allah knows what you reveal and what you conceal.

And if they do come into contact with a women or girl to whom they are not married or related they must not look at her directly and they must make sure their "private parts" are covered.

> 24:30 Tell the believers to cast down their eyes and guard their private parts. This is purer for them. Allah is conversant with what they do.

The alleged indiscretion by Aisha is also, in my estimation, responsible for Allah placing severe restrictions on believing women's freedom of movement; telling them what they could wear and how they must wear it; leaving instructions on the company a woman could keep and why they should cover up "their private parts" and not stamp their feet.

> 24:31 And tell the believing women to cast down their eyes and guard their private parts and not show their finery, except the outward part of it. And let them drape their bosoms with their veils and not show their finery, except to their husbands, their fathers, their husbands' fathers, their sons, the sons of their husbands, their brothers, the sons of their brothers, the sons of their sisters, their women, their maid-servants, the men-followers who have no sexual desire, or infants who have no knowledge of women's sexual parts yet. Let them, also, not stamp their feet, so that what they have concealed of their finery might be known. Repent to Allah, all of you, O believers, that perchance you may prosper.

Allah also has a few instructions that are for His Messenger's wives only. In a book for the ages this seems out of place. The Prophet's wives are in a class by themselves. As befitting their exalted status, if they make a fool of His Messenger again they will suffer double the punishment of an ordinary wife, revelation 33:30, and He will see to it personally.

> 33:28 O Prophet, say to your wives: "If you desire the present life and its finery, so come along that I might provide for you and set you free kindly.

> 33:29 "But if you desire Allah, His Messenger and the life to come, surely Allah has prepared for the beneficent among you a great wage."

> 33:30 O wives of the Prophet, whomever of you commits a flagrant foul act, her punishment will be doubled; and that for Allah is an easy matter.

If the fear of double the punishment for putting His Messenger in an embarrassing situation is not enough, Allah is not beneath offering a little monetary incentive.

> 33:31 Whoever of you obeys Allah and His Messenger and does the righteous deed, We shall pay her wage twice over, and we have prepared for her a generous provision.

Being the wife of God's Messenger may not have been all that fulfilling for some of the women and girls confined to the Prophet's household for Allah to admonish them to "not be abject in speech" e.g. expressing hopelessness when talking about their lives with the greatest of them all. They may have even expressed a wish that their husband might give them their freedom, which would explain why Allah revealed that "he in whose heart is a sickness may covet you".

Hope springs eternal. The "sickness" alluded to by Allah may simply have been young men expressing the desire that, because a wife of the Prophet expressing a wish to be free of her husband, that they might one day get a share of the Prophet's bounty of beautiful women and girls.

> 33:32 O wives of the Prophet, you are not like any other women. If you are God-fearing, do not be abject in speech, so that he in whose heart is a sickness may covet you, but speak in an honourable way.

Some may have done what young women do when they are
desperate for the attention that an extremely busy older husband may
not have been able to provide, and that is look for validation of their
attractiveness as young women in a young man's eyes. This would
explain Allah's demand that they stay inside and out of sight so as
not to expose their "finery", and keep busy with prayers and giving
"the alms". As to how they could give "the alms" if they were not
allowed to leave the house is problematic. In any event, the extreme
restrictions Allah imposed on His Messenger's females, effectively
making them invisible to the outside world, was not to cause them
hardship, which it obviously did, but to purify them "fully".

> 33:33 Stay in your homes and do not display your finery as
> the pagans of old did: perform the prayer, give the alms
> and obey Allah and His Messenger. Allah only wishes to
> turn away abomination from you and purify you fully. O
> People of the House.

> 33:34 And remember what is recited in your homes of
> Allah's Signs and of wisdom. Indeed, Allah is Subtle, Well-
> Informed.

> 33:35 Men and women who have submitted, believed,
> obeyed, are truthful, steadfast, reverend, giving in charity,
> fasting, guarding their private parts and remembering
> Allah often, Allah has prepared for them forgiveness and a
> great reward.

Because of the beautiful, young Aisha's alleged sexual indiscretion
and Allah's concern about his Messenger being ridiculed for not
being able to control his young brood, women everywhere in the
conservative Muslim world are forced into seclusion to this day.
Allah admonished His Messenger's wives to stay at home, and
conservative Muslim men have been enjoining their wives and
daughters to do the same ever since.

~~~~~~~~~~~~~~~

Allah relaxed his severe dress code for women passed child-bearing
age who had no chance of marriage.

> 24:60 Those women who are past child-bearing and have no
> hope of marriage are not at fault if they take off their outer
> garments, not exhibiting any finery; but to refrain is better
> for them. Allah is All-Hearing, All-Knowing.

He also made an exception to a woman not displaying "her fineries" during hostilities.

> 33:59 O Prophet, tell your wives and daughters and the wives of the believers, to draw their outer garments closer. That is more conducive to them being known and not being injured. Allah is All-Forgiving, Merciful.

The wives of the Prophet, according to Fakhry, are not at fault if they appear unveiled to members of their close family and female slaves. If you are female and Muslim and believe this verse only applied to the wives of the Prophet then you will not feel compelled to cover your face in public, otherwise you have no choice if you don't want Allah to find fault with you.

> 33:55 They (the wives of the Prophet, if they appear unveiled) are not at fault regarding their fathers, their sons, their brothers, their brothers' sons, their sisters' sons' or their wives and what their right hands possess; so fear Allah. Surely, Allah is Witness of everything.

The Lost Verse

Those who do not respond to insults with an insult of their own; those who prostrate themselves or stand up night and day in prayer; those who plead not to be sent to Hell; those who spend their money wisely; those who believe in Allah and only Allah and repentant murderers, but perhaps not adulterers (revelation 25:68), will be given a shot at Paradise.

25:63 And the servants of the Compassionate who walk in the land gently and, if the ignorant address them, they say: "Peace."

25:64 And those who pass the night prostrating themselves to their Lord or standing up.

25:65 And those who say: "Lord, divert from us the agony of Hell"; but its agony is unavoidable punishment.

25:66 Wretched it is as a final resort and resting-place!

25:67 And those who, when they spend, do not squander or stint, but chose a middle course between that.

25:68 And those who do not call upon any other god than Allah, and do not kill the soul which Allah forbade, except justly; and they do not commit adultery. He who does that shall meet with retribution.

25:69 Punishment shall be doubled for him on the Day of Resurrection (Judgement Day) and he will dwell forever in it down-trodden;

25:70 Except for him who repents, believes and does the righteous deed. Those Allah will change their evil deeds into good deeds. Allah is ever All-Forgiving, Merciful.

25:71 He who repents and does the righteous deed returns to Allah unhampered.

Murder and adultery in the same revelation should give you an idea of how seriously Allah takes infidelity. Still, there are no revelations about an adulteress being put to death in the entire "official" Koran. This, however, does not mean that adulteresses and sometimes adulterers, get off lightly. In revelation 4:15 Allah recommends the very harsh punishment of confining the adulteress to her home until she died.

> 4:15 As for those of your women who commit adultery, call four witnesses from your own against them; and if they testify then detain them in the houses till death overtakes them or Allah opens another way for them.

If two men were found guilty of adultery the punishment was or could be much less severe and a slow, lingering death unlikely. Why two men? Fakhry does not provide any explanation for his additional text.

> 4:16 If two [men] of you commit it, punish them both. If they repent and mend their ways, then leave them alone. Allah is truly All-Forgiving, Merciful.

Men were to be forgiven their adulterous transgressions but not women. Perhaps realising the unfairness of it all Allah changed his mind ... *maybe*?

Verse 4:15 was later abrogated (annulled) and replaced by another where the woman's punishment was greatly reduced and men were now also susceptible to being found guilty of adultery and suffering the same reduced punishment as the female partner in an adulteress affair.

THE LIGHT

24 An-Nûr

*In the Name of Allah,
the Compassionate, the Merciful*

> 24:1 A Surah that We have sent down and stipulated, and We have sent down in it clear revelations, that perchance you might remember.

> 24:2 The adulteress and the adulterer, whip each one of them a hundred lashes; and let no pity move you in Allah's religion, regarding them; if you believe in Allah and the

Hereafter. And let a group of believers witness their punishment.

Adulterers can only marry each other or an unbeliever.

24:3 The adulterer shall marry none but an adulteress or an idolatress; and the adulteress none shall marry her but an adulterer or idolater. That has been forbidden the believers.

The punishment for un-corroborated accusation of sexual impropriety against an unmarried woman was only slightly less painful than being found guilty of adultery.

24:4 Those who accuse chaste women, then cannot bring four witnesses, whip them eighty lashes, and do not ever accept their testimony. For those are the wicked sinners.

24:5 Except for those who repent afterwards and mend their ways. For Allah is surely All-Forgiving, Merciful.

A wife accused of adultery by her husband could avoid the public whipping altogether by calling her husband a liar.

24:6 And those who accuse their wives and have no witnesses except themselves, the testimony of one of them shall be to swear by Allah four times that he is truthful.

24:7 The fifth time shall be Allah's Curse on him if he is a liar.

24:8 And her swearing four times by Allah that he is a liar will ward off punishment from her.

24:9 And the fifth time will be that Allah's Wrath be upon her, if he (her husband) is truthful.

A Lost Verse Remembered

If Allah says a public whipping is the punishment for adultery and a wife can avoid even that punishment by calling her husband a liar, why are women accused of adultery still susceptible to being stoned to death in countries where the Koran is the law? And, why do some countries where the Koran is the law, favour the execution of alleged adulteresses and girls, such as sixteen-year-old Atefah Sahaaleh, who was hanged in a public square in the Iranian city of Neka in 2004 for having pre-marital sex? Is it because the Prophet was in favour of stoning women for adultery?

Malik related to me from Yaqub ibn Zayd ibn Talha from his father Zayd ibn Talha that Abdullah ibn Abi Mulayka informed him that a woman came to the Messenger of Allah, may Allah bless him and grant him peace, and informed him that she had committed adultery and was pregnant. The Messenger of Allah, may Allah bless him and grant him peace, said to her, "Go away until you give birth." When she had given birth, she came to him. The Messenger of Allah, may Allah bless him and grant him peace, said to her, "Go away until you have suckled and weaned the baby." When she had weaned the baby, she came to him. He said, "Go and entrust the baby to someone." She entrusted the baby to someone and then came to him. He gave the order and she was stoned. (Al-Muwatta)

Syed Shahabuddin writing in the Milli Gazette, Indian Muslim's leading English newspaper reminds us that that flogging is the punishment for adultery, not stoning and the Koran is the final authority, even the Prophet could not substitute his own opinion. So why does Islamic Law, in some jurisdictions, give precedence to the example of the Prophet instead of the Koran?

According to Shahabuddin this is because "some [Islamic] scholars support 'Rajm' (stoning) by attributing a statement to the second Caliph Umar (second successor to the Prophet Muhammad) that a revelation on the subject had been received but had been lost." In a hadith collected by the famous Sunni scholar Ibn Hanbal the verse was eaten by a goat.

[Narrated 'Aisha] "The verse of the stoning and of suckling an adult ten times were revealed, and they were (written) on a paper and kept under my bed. When the messenger of Allah expired and we were preoccupied with his death, a goat entered and ate away the paper."

So there you have it. When you hear of a woman being stoned or murdered for committing adultery or for having pre-marital relations in conservative Muslim jurisdictions such as Iran, Nigeria or Saudi Arabia the justification just might be this lost verse of the Koran. Shahabuddin, always helpful, also explains why it is always women who get stoned even though the punishment is supposed to apply equally to both sexes.

"Apart from the brutality of the 'Rajm' (stoning), repugnant to conscience, here is an element of gender injustice in the operation of the traditional law which allows the male partner to get off scot-free, even if he has coerced and raped the female. If the woman lodges a complaint, her complaint is taken as a testimony against herself and, therefore, amounts to admission and requires no further evidence while it is necessary to get 4 witnesses against the man. Also the woman may bear a child, as in Amina's case (Amina Lawal was sentenced to death by stoning by a Nigerian Islamic Sharia Court. Amina had an 8 month old daughter), which is admitted as evidence of zena (guilt) against the woman. Man suffers from no such disability."

~~~~~~~~~~~~~~~~

Ali, the Prophet's cousin and son-in-law, during the discussions concerning Aisha's suspected adulterous one-night stand (see *The Perfect Wife - A Child Bride's Indiscretion*) told his father-in-law that "Allah has not placed any limits on the choice of a wife. They are plentiful" which would suggest that Ali, who was never a fan of Aisha, favoured that she be stoned.

This has led to speculation that Aisha deliberately got rid of the revelation pertaining to stoning a wife for adultery, after her husband passed away, to avoid being stoned should Ali convinced the Prophet's successor to do what the God's Messenger would not do while he was alive.

The Satanic Verses

Pre-Islamic Arabs worshipped three goddesses, al-Lat, al-Uzza, and Manat who they believed to be the daughters of the moon god "al-Ilah" (Allah). Pre-Islamic Arabs had no problems with a spiritual existence that included gods and goddesses. The Prophet's tribe, the Quraysh, used to chant, as they circumambulated the Ka'ba, "Al-Lat, and al-Uzza and Manat, the third, the other; indeed these are exalted gharaniq (cranes); let us hope for their intercession." (*F. E. Peters, The Hajj, p 3-41*)

The Meccans, when the Prophet showed up with his army, gave up without a fight after God's Messenger assured them that Allah, in two revelations, had informed him that He had no objections to the Meccans continuing to worship al-Lat, al-Uzza, and Manat after they became Muslims. These revelations are what are known as the *Satanic Verses.*

These are the exalted cranes (al-Lat, al-Uzza, and Manat)

Whose intercession [with Allah] is to be hoped for.

The next day, after he had complete control of their city, the Prophet told the Meccans that it was all the devil's doing; that Satan had intruded on his conversations with Allah the previous night, and in the morning Allah had set him straight and al-Lat, al-Uzza, and Manat were history and the verses the Prophet had received the previous night were stricken from the Koran.

22:52 We have not sent a Messenger or Prophet before you but when he recited the Devil would intrude into his recitation. Yet Allah annuls what the Devil had cast. Then Allah establishes His Revelations. Allah is All-Knowing and Wise.

How could the Devil do that? Because Allah let him, for His usual somewhat convoluted reasons!

22:53: So as to make what Satan casts a temptation to those in whose hearts there is a sickness, and to those whose hearts are hard. The wrongdoers are indeed in profound discord!

22:54 And so that those who have been given the knowledge might understand that it is the truth from your Lord and so believe in it. Then their hearts will submit to it. Allah will certainly guide the believers to a straight path.

Even if it was His doing i.e. He allowed the devil to intrude on His conversations, Allah is incensed that anyone would associate Him with females whether they be goddesses daughters, even angels.

53:19 Have you, then, seen al-Lat and al-'Uzza?

53:20 And Manat, the third one, the other?

53:21 Do you have the male and He has the female?

53:22 That indeed is an unjust division.

53:23 These are mere names you (*Meccan unbelievers*) and your fathers have named, for which Allah did not send down any authority. They only follow conjecture and what the souls desire; yet Guidance (*the Qur'an*) has come to them from their Lord.

53:24 Or will man have whatever he wishes?

16:57 And they ascribe to Allah daughters [glory be to Him!], but to themselves what they desire (sons).

16:58 And if the birth of a daughter is announced to any of them, his face turns black, and he is enraged.

16:59 He hides from the people on account of the evil news broken to him; should he keep it in humiliation or bury it in the ground? Evil is what they judge!

16:60 As for those who do not believe in the Hereafter, theirs is the evil exemplar; but Allah's is the sublime exemplar. He is the Almighty, the Wise.

16:61 Were Allah to take mankind to task for their wrongdoing, He would not leave upon it (the earth) a single creature; but He reprieves them until an appointed term.

Then, when their term comes, they will not delay nor advance it a single hour.

16:62 And they ascribe to Allah what they themselves dislike (daughters). Their tongues utter the lie that theirs will be the best reward. There is no doubt that the Fire awaits them, and that they will be left [there].

Verse 17:40, which follows, is doubly confusing since angels *have no gender*, although they do take the male form, minus the genitalia, to facilitate communications with humans.

17:40 Has your Lord, then, favoured you with sons and taken to Himself females from among the angels? Surely, you are uttering a monstrous thing.

If you do not believe in the Hereafter you are an unbeliever; and only an unbeliever would give angels female names (give them a gender, and a female one at that), revelation 53:27, knowing Allah's low opinion of the fair sex and His high regard for His angels.

53:25 For to Allah belongs the last and the first life.

53:26 How many an angel is there in heavens whose intercession avails nothing, except after Allah gives leave to whoever He wishes and is well-pleased with.

53:27 Those who do not believe in the Hereafter will surely give the angels the names of females.

53:28 Yet, they have no knowledge thereof. They only follow conjecture, but conjecture avails nothing regarding truth.

53:29 So turn away from him who has given up Our Reminder (*the Qur'an*) and only desire the present life.

53:30 That is their attainment in knowledge. Your Lord indeed knows better than those who have strayed from His Path, and He knows better those who are well-guided.

For one brief shining moment, because of the alleged intervention by Satan, Allah had female partners. Just imagine what Islam would have been like if Allah had acknowledged needing the company of females, whether they be goddesses or mortals. With females for company would Allah have been such a vengeful god, so easily irritated, so quick to kill and terrorize? I don't think so.

Had Allah acknowledged that daughters were just as valuable as sons instead of being insulted that some would attribute themselves sons and to Him females, would women in many countries where the Koran is the law be so harshly treated. Probably not. The denial of the existence of al-Lat, al-Uzza, and Manat marked the end of the Arab civilization of which historian Robert Montagne wrote (my translation) "I am not aware in the entire history of civilisation of a more gracious, more loving, more vibrant society than that of the Arabs before Islam."

The Cult of Masculinity

Misogyny (hatred of or hostility towards women) is perhaps too strong a term, yet a prejudicial view of women is perhaps not strong enough when describing Allah's attitude towards women, an attitude largely shared by His Messenger.

The vehemence that Allah demonstrates towards females may just be an extreme manifestation of the cult of masculinity. The ultimate expression of this male adoration cult was everywhere evident in pagan Arabia where sons were cherished and daughters barely tolerated until a male heir was produced. The whole Arab patronymic naming nomenclature (a part of a personal name is based on the name of one's father) rests on a father being able to trace his ancestry through his father's name (it is expressly forbidden to use a mother or daughter's name to trace your lineage). That is why today, as it was then, Arab names often contain the conjunctions ibn/ben meaning *son of*, or Abu meaning *father of*.

Allah's extreme reaction to being associated with females may also have had something to do with His Messenger not fathering any sons that survived beyond infancy[16]. For this failure the Prophet was often taunted and ridiculed by his enemies who would openly wondered why God had not favoured His greatest Messenger with sons. Both the Prophet and his Benefactor may have seen this inability to father healthy sons as just another of women's many

---

[16] In the surah *Abundance* Allah makes an indirect reference to His Messenger's son who died in infancy.

108:1 We have surely given you abundance;

108: 2 So pray to your Lord and offer in sacrifice.

108:3 Indeed, your chief hater is the real childless (the reference is to Al-'Aas Ibn Wa'il who chided Muhammad upon the death of his son)

failings and both may not have wished to associate themselves too closely with so obviously flawed creatures.

Women and What It
Means To Be Civilized

The clash we are witnessing around the world is not a clash
of religions or a clash of civilization. It is a clash between
civilization and backwardness, between the civilized and
the primitive, between rationality and barbarity. It is a clash
between freedom and oppression, between democracy and
dictatorship. It is a clash between human rights, on one
hand and the violation of these rights on the other. It is a
clash between those who treat women like beasts, and those
who treat them like human beings ...

*Wafa Sultan, outspoken Syrian-American woman during a debate
broadcast on Al-jazeera.*

Males are using women's ignorance of the Koran against
them. This has to change starting with women because it is
believing women who transmit this misogynous male
interpretation of the Koran from generation to generation.

*Asma Lamrabet, hematologist, author and Muslim activist during
an interview on Radio-Canada (my translation).*

If women are being treated less then equitably in societies and
households around the world which accept the Koran as God's words
and the Prophet as their guide, which of the two sexes is most
responsible for the propagation of values that, according to Wafa
Sultan, reduce women to the equivalent of a beast of burden?
Perhaps, not surprisingly, it is women, with women like Wafa Sultan
and Asma Lamrabet being the exception. The biggest obstacle for
Muslim women to bettering their lot in life has not been men but
other women. It is mostly opposition from their own sex that has
made the struggle for equality with Muslim men so difficult.

This opposition takes two forms: in the West it is Muslim
women who act as apologists for Allah and His Messenger's low

opinion of their sex; in societies dominated by the Koran, it is the
mothers. It is mainly Muslim mothers who are tasked with the
responsibility of ensuring that Muslim women remain inferior and
are accepting of this inferior status that makes them completely
dependent on the men who "own" them; men to whom the Koran
grants dictatorial powers over every facet of their lives including their
sex life.

In traditional Islamic societies it is the mother who is responsible
for the upbringing of sons until they reach the age of seven or so, and
daughters until they have reached puberty. As explained by Bernard
Lewis in his book *What Went Wrong,* published just after the attacks of
September 11, 2001 in New York; "… it is these downtrodden, mainly
illiterate mothers that are entrusted with the crucial early years of the
upbringing of the other half."

The traditions of conservative Islam that condemn believing
women to a subservient mostly miserable existence – apart from the
clerics and teachers who drill the content of the Koran into a child's
mind – are largely sustained and transmitted from generation to
generation by other women.

Not only are mothers largely responsible for Muslim men's
superior, condescending attitude towards women, they are also
responsible for raising their daughters into accepting their inferior
almost slave-like status as being the natural order of things. Like
other neat little god-made constructs of Islam, it is to be admired if
only for the ingenuous way Allah and His Messenger manoeuvre
Muslim women into being an enemy of their sex.

Women of Islam

While the poor, "downtrodden, mainly illiterate mothers" found in
societies where the Koran rules may be excused for their role in
ensuring that their daughters will always be inferior to men, what is
the excuse of Muslim women in the West who know better, or who
should know better?

Whether they do so out of conviction or have been pressed into
service by their father, husband or brother, it is women in the West in
general and in Canada in particular, who have become spokespersons
for the voice and face of so-called moderate, modern Islam. A modern
view that still maintains that the Koran is the literal Word of God,
and that Allah's and His Messenger's questionable views on
everything from women to murdering those who would leave the

faith, are beyond reproach. The latest manifestation of this self-defeating phenomenon in Canada was during the so-called "cartoon protest."

It was mainly Muslim women, acting as spokespersons for the Canadian Islamic community, who appeared on television, with stern Muslim men looking on, and demanded that those who dared to publish mostly innocent caricatures of the Prophet Muhammad be prosecuted. It is women such as these who perpetuate the myth of the Prophet's infallibility; conferring god-like immunity to an extraordinary, but still fallible human being.

This newfound public role for Muslim women in the West is in sharp contrast to the other public affirmation of Koranic values; the now regular television broadcast. You will not find many women here. Only in extraordinary circumstances are women allowed to preach to the faithful, for example, the audience is exclusively female and a male cannot be found.

Muslim women in the West who simply parrot Allah's male-centered, misogynous point of view, have abrogated their responsibility to elevate the debate in favour of equality for their sex. They are selling out their sisters in Afghanistan, Iran, Saudi Arabia, Pakistan, Nigeria, Somalia ... by promoting in a society that considers them equal, a prejudiced view of women that, if widely accepted, would reduce their status to that of their sisters living in obscurity in male-dominated societies where the Koran is supreme.

It is also believing women who are largely responsible, not only for the intellectual but physical mutilation of their daughters. The intellectual mutilation begins with the force feeding of the Koran and Allah's prejudiced opinion that males are superior and more valuable than females. This cerebral mutilation is done mainly to please their god, the physical mutilation out of fear of displeasing the men in their family, their clan or their tribe, who, like Allah and His Messenger are obsessed with virgins[17].

It is mainly the mother's responsibility to ensure that her daughters remain virgins until her husband can arrange an advantageous marriage to a cousin or another close relative. For a daughter to lose her virginity before marriage is to bring disgrace and dishonour to the entire family and reducing her net worth to next to

---

[17] We find this obsession with virgins in the practice where the bride in an Islamic marriage must submit to total body epilation, except for her eye brows, which are only thinned, and the hair on her head.

nothing. The fear of disgracing their families drives many mothers in traditional Islamic societies, mainly in Africa where the practice originated, to have their daughters undergo a procedure called female circumcision. Unlike male circumcision, female circumcision is much more brutal and is not done out of mostly hygienic considerations as it is for males. As explained by Ayaan Hirsi Ali whose grand-mother arranged for her to suffer the procedure.

> ...Islam demands that your enter marriage as a virgin. The virgin dogma is safeguarded by locking girls up in their homes and sewing their outer labia together. Female circumcision serves two purposes; the clitoris is removed in order to reduce the woman's sexuality, and the labia are sewn up in order to guarantee her virginity.

Hirsi Ali, The Caged Virgin, p.76.

Women of Sumer

The *Epic of Gilgamesh* pre-dates the Hebrew Bible by at least two-thousand years, the Koran by an additional one-thousand-five-hundred years – more or less. It was carved into clay tablets at the dawn of Western written history in ancient Sumeria (Sumer). In it you will find a story about the great flood and the Garden of Eden. How would Islam, which contains variations of the same stories as can be found in the *Epic of Gilgamesh* and later in the Bible reconcile the two?

The Koran contains references to twenty five prophets who came before the Prophet Muhammad and it is clear that there are many more. In one *tradition of the Prophet*, more than 124,000 prophets were sent by Allah before He got fed up with His Message being badly transmitted or misunderstood and decided to send His last and greatest Messenger, the Prophet Muhammad

Believers would maintain that the author of *Gilgamesh* was probably a prophet who was misquoted or who misunderstood Allah's Message. For instance, how could someone possibly write that it was a woman who gave birth to humanity not a man; or that it is a woman, as described in the following excerpt from that heroic poem, to whom we are indebted for the wisdom with which she endowed man and which allowed civilization to blossom (from a translation by Stephanie Dalley):

Shambat loosened her undergarments, opened her legs and
    he took in her attractions.
She did not pull away. She took wind of him.
Spread open her garments and he lay upon her.
She did for him, the primitive man, as women do.
His love-making he lavished upon her.
For six days and seven nights Enkidu was aroused and
    poured himself into Shambat.
When he was sated with her charms,
He set his face towards the open country of his cattle.
The gazelles saw Enkidu and scattered.
The cattle of open country kept away from his body.
For Enkidu had become smooth; his body was too clean.
His legs, which used to keep pace with his cattle, were at a
    standstill.
Enkidu had been diminished, he could not run as before.
Yet he had acquired judgement, had become wiser.

For the Sumerians it was the goddess Aruru, the mother goddess, who created Enkidu from clay – the Bible and the Koran would give that role to a man. For the Sumerians, women were a civilizing influence; for the illiterate desert tribesmen who would usurp her role in the creation accounts, she became the seductress, the harlot who caused mankind to be expelled from Paradise.

For the men and women of Sumer, their cities were Paradise. For the people of Sumer it was also women as life givers, homemakers and lovers who made this sedentary, civilized lifestyle possible, desirable and enjoyable. For the tribesmen of the desert, trapped and fighting for survival beneath a monotonous, unchanging blue sky and a blaring scorching sun on a sea of dust and sand, the cities of Sumer would also have been seen as Paradise. Allah's description of Paradise, as an oasis with buildings and women as pleasure providers, almost fits the description of Sumerian cities and their female inhabitants, with the exception that in Sumer, *women were not second class citizens.*

Why would desert tribesmen, who would adapt, if not pervert many of the events described in the *Epic of Gilgamesh,* including the story of the meeting between Shambat and Enkidu blame women for mankind's exile from Paradise? The seduction of Enkidu by Shambat was seen as a good thing by the people of Sumer; a wild, roving man is civilized by being intimate with a woman.

For the people of Sumer being "civilized" meant acquiring wisdom; becoming capable of exercising judgement, of assessing situations or circumstances shrewdly and logically and drawing your own reasonable conclusions. For the illiterate, fatalistic tribesmen of the deserts of the Middle East whose very existence was constantly being tested by elements over which they had no control, which they believed was God's way of trying their faith, this had to appear like blasphemy. Paradise was to be denied mankind because a woman was foolish enough to endow a man with god-like qualities. For their jealous, vengeful god this had to be unacceptable.

The Koran with its meticulous instructions as to what a believer may or may not do; what a believer may think or say was perhaps the primitive tribesman's way of using the invention of writing to establish eternal, unchanging limits on mankind's imagination and freewill in the hope of convincing God to let man back into Sumer, back into Paradise.

Writing as Allah revealed in verses from surah 96, *The Clot* made man arrogant, thinking himself self-sufficient. This was not why He taught man how to write. He taught man how to write, not to make him more self-sufficient, but less, by having him write down His unchanging instructions as to how He expected man to behave and how He was to be worshipped. Instructions which He expected to be followed to the literal letter or man will have to answer to Him to Whom all of mankind must eventually return.

96:3 Read by your Most Generous Lord,

96:4 Who taught <u>by the pen</u>.

96:5 He thought man what he did not know.

96:6 Yet, man will, indeed wax arrogant;

96:7 For he thinks himself self-sufficient.

96:8 Surely, unto your Lord is the ultimate return.

It was the Sumerians who more than five millennia ago, first carved the written word on clay tablets. According to Thomas Cahill, the period before the invention of writing saw an "explosion of technological creativity on a scale that would not be matched until the nineteenth and twentieth century of our era." Writing may have been a result of mankind's need to record this leap which memory could no longer be counted on to chronicle or manage. Civilization could not progress any further without the means of recording civilization's accomplishments for future generations to build on.

The society that invented writing worshipped many goddesses. The greatest goddess of all, Ishtar, the goddess of love and war, was worshipped by the people of the city of Uruk, perhaps the earliest settlement to deserve the name of city. It was in this ancient Mesopotamian city, on the shore of the Euphrates River that the first words written five thousand years ago on clay tablets were found. If it was not a woman who imagined those first words then it was her civilizing influence which allowed the written word to be imagined in the first place.

Civilization in the Balance

Women have been deciding the fate of civilizations since the dawn of written history and probably long before that, and they will continue to be largely responsible for the fate of humanity. The women of Sumer rocked the cradle of Western Civilization and nurtured it through its formative years until the Greeks and Romans of antiquity came along and put into words and deeds what it meant to be *western* and *civilized*. For the Greeks of antiquity, in particular, to be civilized meant subscribing to democratic ideals; appreciating that liberty is humanity's most precious possession; accepting that ethics and morality can come from within and that the search for the truth is a never ending quest and a noble calling in and of itself.

Following in the footsteps of the Greeks and Romans came the philosophical movement of the 18th century, *The Enlightenment*, that emphasized the use of reason to question accepted doctrines and traditions; and before that, *The Renaissance* which marked the end of the Catholic Church's dominance in Europe allowing for a flowering of the arts and sciences. Today, competing with these ideas of what it means to be civilized is a child-like view of the world that begins and ends with the Koran. The Koran is not so much a philosophy as a set of rules, formulated by a child-like-mind; rules which embody a child's certainty in having absolute knowledge of the world around him and a child's intolerance of others who won't play the game by his rules.

To accept this child-like-view of the world is to deny Western Civilization and all its accomplishments. This child-like view of the universe saw writing as a way of putting a limit on what people can imagine. This child-like view now competes with the grown-up view of the people of Sumer who invented writing as a means to expand the capabilities of the human mind not to limit them; who invented writing so as to allow future generations to build on, to go beyond, to question what their ancestors had imagined.

The women of Sumer gave birth to Western Civilization. The women of Islam, who are a child's first acquaintance with the Koran and the narrow limits it places on the imagination, may bring it to an end. The Koran, taken literally kills the imagination allowing insanity to settle in. Will these mainly "illiterate and downtrodden mothers" that are entrusted with the crucial early years of a child's upbringing – invisible to the outside world courtesy of a prudish, insecure, misogynous God – even be aware of what they have done.

Appendices

Rukaya Saves the Prophet
Or Rockin the Ka'ba

> 2:114 And who is more unjust than those (*the Meccans*) who prohibit mentioning of Allah in His mosques, and who even seek to destroy them. Those people should not have been allowed to enter them except in fear. For them there is a disgrace in this world, and terrible punishment in the Hereafter.

Worshipping at the Ka'ba was not always the somber, ritualized spectacle you have today, during the Hajj for instance. The revelation pertaining to pre-Islamic worship at the Ka'ba is part of a series of revelation which begin with a verse about Allah outscheming (sic) the Meccans and thereby saving his Prophet's life, but not from being expelled from Mecca as you will soon discover.

> 8:30 And [remember (Muhammad)] when the unbelievers plotted against you, so as to confine you, kill you or expel you. They schemed and Allah schemed, but Allah is the Best of schemers.

There were at least two attempts on the Prophet's life during his time in Mecca. One rather disgusting attempt occurred about three years after he received the first communication from the Angel Gabriel.

He was kneeling in prayer at the Ka'ba when a fellow by the name of Abu Jahl came up behind him with the stomach of a dead camel which he placed like a sac on top of the Prophet's head intending to suffocate him. Somehow, Abu Jahl managed to get God's Messenger completely inside the camel's stomach which he then sealed with the intestines of the animal.

None of the men who witnessed the attempted murder intervened; but one woman rushed to the house of the Prophet and told Rukaya what was being done to her father. She rushed to the Ka'ba and liberated her dad from the camel's stomach saving his life.

Tiring of listening to the Prophet insult their ancestors for worshipping idols – the last straw was probably God's Messenger's insistence that their forefathers were burning in Hell because they died unbelievers and that is where they would end up if they followed their ancestor's example – the Meccans banned the Prophet and his followers from the Ka'ba.

The believers defied the ordinance, prompting the Meccans, in 616, to send them all into exile. The next time the Prophet will enter Mecca, it will be as its conqueror.

God's Messenger, or perhaps his followers, may have wondered why Allah did not punish those who had tried to kill him, including attempting to suffocate him using a dead camel's stomach. Allah had a ready answer:

> 8:33 And Allah did not wish to punish them while you (Muhammad) were in their midst, and Allah was not going to punish them while they were asking for forgiveness.

Some Meccans obviously regretted being part of the plot to kill the Prophet or not coming to the aid of God's Messenger and asked for forgiveness. As to the believers being barred from the Ka'ba, the unbelievers had no right!

> 8:34 And what excuse do they have that Allah should not punished them, when they bar people from the Sacred Mosque[18], although they were not its guardians? Its guardians are only those who fear Allah; but most of them do not know.

And what was it like worshipping at the Sacred Mosque before the believers became its guardians and it was the unbelievers who were denied admittance.

> 8:35 Their prayer at the House (the Ka'ba) is nothing but whistling and clapping; so taste the punishment for your disbelief.

~~~~~~~~~~~~~~~~

Allah's claim notwithstanding – Rukaya could have been His instrument - the Prophet owed his life to a brave female while males

---

[18] The enclosure surrounding the Ka'ba.

stood by and watched. It was also a woman, his first wife Khadijah, whose faith in her husband and wealth ensured his success as a merchant and later financed his activities as a budding prophet. Knowing this, it is even harder to fathom Allah and His Messenger's distrust and disparagement of females and the restrictions they have placed on their freedom of movement and action.

If the interdiction against women leaving the house unaccompanied by a close male relative or guardian had been in effect when the attempted suffocation of God's Messenger's was made, the Prophet's *progress* would have come to an abrupt halt.

What Aisha Saw

"O enwrapped one" is how Allah refers to His Messenger in revelation 73:1. Fakhry, in a footnote, explains that "this refers to Muhammad, who used to be 'wrapped up' when the Koran was imparted to him by the Angel Gabriel".

THE ENWRAPPED

73 Al-Muzzamil

*In the Name of Allah,
the Compassionate, the Merciful*

73:1 O enwrapped one,

73:2 Keep vigil throughout the night, except for a little while;

73:3 Half of it, or a little less;

73:4 Or add a little thereto and chant the Qur'an loudly.

73:5 Indeed, We shall deliver unto you a weighty discourse.

73:6 Surely, the early hours of the night are more onerous and more amenable to straight talk.

73:7 You have during the day a long-drawn business.

73:8 Remember the name of your Lord and devote yourself fully to Him.

....

In verse 73:20, a lengthy mishmash of a revelation which concludes *The Enwrapped One* Allah reveals that His Messenger may not have been alone; that other mortals i.e. "a group of followers", waited with His Messenger for Gabriel to bring down His latest instructions for mankind.

Except for perhaps Aisha, and she did not see much and got

punched in the chest for her honesty in telling her husband what she did not see, none of these "followers" has ever come forward and claimed to have been with the Prophet during any meeting with the angel Gabriel.

> 73:20 Your Lord knows that you keep vigil a little less than two-thirds of the night, and a half or a third thereof, together with a group of your followers. Allah determines the measure of a night and day; He knows that you will not keep it all, and so He has absolved you. Read, then, what you can of the Qur'an. He knows that there will be, among you, sick people and others who journey in the land, seeking part of Allah's Bounty, and still others who fight for the Cause of Allah. Recite, then, what you can of it, perform the prayer, give the alms and lend Allah a fair loan[19]. Whatever good you forward for your soul's sake, you shall find it with Allah growing into greater good and a greater wage. Seek Allah's forgiveness; Allah is indeed All-Forgiving, All-Merciful.

What Aisha saw is recorded in an hadith. Sunni Islam considers the hadiths collected by six men – al-Bukhari, Sahih Muslim, At-Tirmidi, Ibn Majah, Abu Dawood and An-Nisa'i – as the "six canonical collections." They have the force of law. The following hadith # 2127 is from *The Book of Prayers* (Kitab Al-Salat)' of Sahih Muslim; it begins with a typical introduction with the narrator identifying himself, and if it is hearsay, as most are, who he heard it from, followed by some atypical comments from his audience:

> Muhammad b. Qais said (to the people): Should I not narrate to you (a hadith of the Holy Prophet) on my authority and on the authority of my mother? We thought that he meant the mother who had given him birth. He

---

[19] Fakhry, in a footnote, explains that this expression means "spend money in His way." There are at least five revelations about giving Allah a fair loan and these verses are often used in fundraising campaigns. Example from a fundraising letter:

"I am writing to you on behalf of Canberra Islamic Centre (CIC) Executive Committee in the holy month of Ramadan to seek your financial support and prayer for ongoing Islamic project in our National Capital ... Your donation is an investment in the path of Islam that will benefit to the Muslim generations in Canberra/Australia. As mentioned in the Holy Qur'an (64.17) 'If you lend Allah a fair loan, He will multiply it for you and forgive you. Allah is All Grateful, All Clement.'"

(Muhammad b. Qais) then reported that it was 'A'isha who had narrated this: Should I not narrate to you about myself and about the Messenger of Allah (may peace be upon him)? We said: Yes.

From Aisha we learn that it all started when she joined her husband for an intimate moment, after which, thinking she is asleep God's Messenger leaves her side.

> She said: When it was my turn for Allah's Messenger (may peace be upon him) to spend the night with me, he turned his side, put on his mantle and took off his shoes and placed them near his feet, and spread the corner of his shawl on his bed and then lay down till he thought that I had gone to sleep. He took hold of his mantle slowly and put on the shoes slowly, and opened the door and went out and then closed it lightly.

Aisha is not asleep and decides to follow the Prophet outside where she observes God's Messenger doing hand gestures, after which they both return to the house; Aisha rushing ahead of her husband and hopping into bed hoping he is none the wiser.

> I covered my head, put on my veil and tightened my waist wrapper, and then went out following his steps till he reached Baqi'. He stood there and he stood for a long time. He then lifted his hands three times, and then returned and I also returned. He hastened his steps and I also hastened my steps. He ran and I too ran. He came (to the house) and I also came (to the house). I, however, preceded him and I entered (the house), and as I lay down in the bed, he (the Holy Prophet) entered the (house), and said:

The Prophet is no fool, he notices she is out of breath and asks the obvious question; and she better tell him the truth because if she does not, Allah will tell on her.

> Why is it, O 'A'isha, that you are out of breath? I said: There is nothing. He said: Tell me or the Subtle and the Aware would inform me.

Aisha tells whatever she tells God's Messenger, swearing it is the truth, and this is when her husband strikes her.

I said: Messenger of Allah, may my father and mother be ransom for you, and then I told him (the whole story). He said: Was it the darkness (of your shadow) that I saw in front of me? I said: Yes. He struck me on the chest which caused me pain, and then said: Did you think that Allah and His Apostle would deal unjustly with you? She said: Whatsoever the people conceal, Allah will know it.

At this point, the Prophet feels compel to explain to an obviously skeptical young woman why she did not observe him and the angel Gabriel in animated conversation; one of the reason being that she was not appropriately dressed.

He said: Gabriel came to me when you saw me. He called me and he concealed it from you. I responded to his call, but I too concealed it from you (for he did not come to you), as you were not fully dressed. I thought that you had gone to sleep, and I did not like to awaken you, fearing that you may be frightened.

The hadith ends with the Prophet, on Gabriel's order, instructing his wife to go to a graveyard, where he will join her later, and pray for the dead as penance for having spied on her husband.

He (Gabriel) said: Your Lord has commanded you to go to the inhabitants of Baqi' (to those lying in the graves) and beg pardon for them. I said: Messenger of Allah, how should I pray for them (How should I beg forgiveness for them)? He said: Say, Peace be upon the inhabitants of this city (graveyard) from among the Believers and the Muslims, and may Allah have mercy on those who have gone ahead of us, and those who come later on, and we shall, God willing, join you.

The Reward of the Female
Suicide Bomber

What rewards can a female jihadist expect from Allah for fighting and dying to extend his dominion on earth? Again, according to David Cook, a question was posed on the Hamas website by a prospective female suicide bomber as to what are the "rewards for a female martyr." Would she get the equivalent of the male suicide bombers who are promised a "fairly extensive harem of women in return for martyrdom."

> [Question] I wanted to ask: what is the reward of a female martyr who performs a martyrdom operation; does she marry 72 of the houris?

> [Answer] ... the female martyr gains the same rewards as does the male, with the exception of this one aspect [the *houris*], so that the female martyr will be with the same husband with whom she dies. "And those who have believed and their progeny, followed them in belief. We shall join their progeny to them. We shall not deprive them of any of their work; every man shall be bound by what he has earned" [52:21]. <u>The one who is martyred and has no husband will be married to one of the people of Paradise.</u>

> *David Cook, Understanding Jihad, p.146*

That would be the same reward – sex with their former spouse after they have been purified (synonyms: cleansed, disinfected, decontaminated...) – that a stay-at-home housewife could expect from Allah, therefore there is nothing to be gained by a chaste girl or a pious married women blowing herself up and killing herself and a bunch of innocent people for Allah.

> 3:15 Say: "Shall I tell you about something better than all that?" For those who are God-fearing, from their Lord are

gardens beneath which rivers flow, and in which they abide forever [along with] purified spouses and Allah's good pleasure. Allah's sees His servants well!

36:55 Today the Companions of Paradise are busy enjoying themselves;

36:56 Together with their spouses they are reclining on couches in the shade.

36:57 Wherein they have fruit, and have all they call for.

36:58 "Peace", uttered by a Merciful Lord.

Sex and the Booty

Booty, which includes the wives and daughters of the unbelievers you killed or enslaved, played a significant part in attracting men to Islam. In making war on the unbelievers Allah reminded the believers not to let the booty distract them from their immediate goal which is shedding the blood of the unbelievers.

> 8:67 It is not up to any Prophet to take captives except after too much blood is shed (after the enemy is hard hit and subdued) in the land. You desire the fleeting goods of this world, but Allah desires the Hereafter, and Allah is Mighty, and Wise.

> 8:68 But for a prior ordinance of Allah, you would have been afflicted on account of what you have taken (an ordinance which made it lawful for Muslims to take spoils and captives) by a terrible punishment.

> 8:69 So eat of the lawful and good things you have taken as booty. Fear Allah; Allah is truly All-Forgiving, Merciful.

It was a given that you could have sex with your female human booty. However, until God's Messenger ruled on the matter, some holy warriors were unsure about whether coitus interruptus was halal.

> Narrated Abu Said Al-Khudri: that while he was sitting with Allah's Apostle he said, "O Allah's Apostle! We get female captives as our share of booty, and we are interested in their prices, what is your opinion about coitus interruptus?" The Prophet said, "Do you really do that? It is better for you not to do it. No soul that which Allah has destined to exist, but will surely come into existence."
> *Bukhari*

Abu Sirma said to Abu Sa'id al Khadri (Allah be pleased with him): 0 Abu Sa'id, did you hear Allah's Messenger (may peace be upon him) mentioning al-'azl? He said: Yes, and added: We went out with Allah's Messenger (may peace be upon him) on the expedition to the Bi'l- Mustaliq and took captive some excellent Arab women; and we desired them, for we were suffering from the absence of our wives, (but at the same time) we also desired ransom for them. So we decided to have sexual intercourse with them but by observing 'azl (Withdrawing the male sexual organ before emission of semen to avoid conception). But we said: We are doing an act whereas Allah's Messenger is amongst us; why not ask him? So we asked Allah's Messenger (may peace be upon him), and he said: It does not matter if you do not do it, for every soul that is to be born up to the Day of Resurrection will be born. *Imam Muslim*

Witches and Sorceresses

Ali Hussain Sibat hosted a popular show broadcast in Arabic from Beirut. On his show he offered advice on a variety of subjects and made predictions about the future. In 2008, he went on pilgrimage to Saudi Arabia, was arrested by the religious police and charged and convicted of sorcery and sentenced to be beheaded.

When it came to the management of women the Prophet really did not leave anything to chance. The relationship between husband and wives decreed by Allah and confirmed by his Messenger in his *Last Sermon* as comparable to that of a prisoner and her jailor: "Treat the women kindly, for verily, they are like prisoners in your house and are incapable of looking after themselves..." is for the believers the recipe for matrimonial harmony. How do you avoid someone tampering with this perfect arrangement? You make it a crime punishable by death for offering advice contrary to the Koran (advice given by a layman being construed as being contrary to the Koran).

I would hazard (his trial was secret) that Ali Hussain Sibat's death sentence was imposed because on his show, he gave advice to married women and speculated on the future of their relationship which, for Allah, is tantamount to practicing the black arts, a crime akin to apostasy. This opinion is based on verse 2:102 and Allah and His Messenger's predilection to want to control every facet of a post-pubescent female's existence.

> 2:101 And when a Messenger came to them from Allah confirming what they had, a group of those who were given the Book (the Torah) cast the Book (Qur'an) of Allah behind their backs, as if they knew nothing;

> 2:102 And they believed what the devils said about Solomon's kingdom. Not that Solomon disbelieved; but the devils did, teaching the people witchcraft and that which was revealed in Babylon to the two angels, Harut and Marut. Yet those two angels did not teach anybody without

saying [to him]: "We are a temptation. So do not disbelieve." Those [who wished] learned from them what would sow discord between man and wife, but could not harm anybody with it (what they had learned), except with Allah's Permission. They learn what harms them and does not profit them. They knew that he who bought it will have no share in the Hereafter. Evil is the price for which they sold themselves, if only they knew.

In the Prophet's time witches were thought to blow into knots to cast spells; another superstition from the Dark Ages which appears to have found its way into the Koran. The second to last surah of the Koran implores Allah to protect men from the evil He admits to creating, including "those who blow into knotted reads", and "from the evil of the envious when he envies."

THE DAYBREAK

113 Al-Falaq

In the Name of Allah,
the Compassionate, the Merciful

113: 1 Say: "I seek refuge with the Lord of the Daybreak,

113:2 "From the evil of what He has created,

113:3 "And the evil of the darkness when it gathers,

113:4 "And the evil of those who blow into knotted reeds (witches or sorceresses),

113:5 "And from the evil of the envious when he envies."

Women on Fire

Of the all the observations the Prophet made about his benefactor's massive torture chamber, the most disturbing has to be that the vast majority of those roasting in His Hell are females – wives and mothers mostly. Allah, the Prophet said, will doom these unfortunate females to an eternity in agony on fire in His Hellhole for not being grateful enough for all the good things their husbands have generously provided them out of the goodness of their heart.

> Narrated Ibn 'Abbas: The Prophet said: "I was shown the Hell-fire and that the majority of its dwellers were women who were ungrateful." It was asked, "Do they disbelieve in Allah?" (or are they ungrateful to Allah?) He replied, "They are ungrateful to their husbands and are ungrateful for the favors and the good (charitable deeds) done to them. *Bukhari*

> Narrated Abu Said Al-Khudri: Once Allah's Apostle went out to the Musalla (to offer the prayer) o 'Id-al- Adha or Al-Fitr prayer. Then he passed by the women and said, "O women! Give alms, as I have seen that the majority of the dwellers of Hellfire were you (women)..." *Bukhari*

> Narrated 'Abdullah bin Abbas: The people say, "O Allah's Apostle! We saw you taking something from your place and then we saw you retreating." The Prophet replied, "I saw Paradise and stretched my hands towards a bunch (of its fruits) and had I taken it, you would have eaten from it as long as the world remains. I also saw the Hell-fire and I had never seen such a horrible sight. I saw that most of the inhabitants were women." The people asked, "O Allah's Apostle! Why is it so?" The Prophet replied, "Because of their ungratefulness." *Bukhari*

Narrated Usama: The Prophet said, "I stood at the gate of Paradise and saw that the majority of the people who entered it were the poor, while the wealthy were stopped at the gate (for the accounts). But the companions of the Fire were ordered to be taken to the Fire. Then I stood at the gate of the Fire and saw that the majority of those who entered it were women." *Bukhari*

Narrated Imran: The Prophet said, "I looked at Paradise and saw that the majority of its residents were the poor; and I looked at the (Hell) Fire and saw that the majority of its residents were women." *Bukhari*

Another reason for so many women in Hell is because even if they have spent an exemplary God-fearing life, if their husbands go to Hell, so do they.

37:22 Gather together those who were wrongdoers, their spouses and what they used to worship;

37:23 Apart from Allah, and lead them to the path of Hell.

www.ingramcontent.com/pod-product-compliance
Lightning Source LLC
Chambersburg PA
CBHW051840040426
42447CB00006B/621